D0225596

OLD AND HOMELESS — DOUBLE-JEOPARDY

KEEP OUT · KEEP OUT

OLD AND HOMELESS—DOUBLE-JEOPARDY

An Overview of Current Practice and Policies

Edited by
Diane Wiatt Rich, Thomas A. Rich,
and Larry C. Mullins

AUBURN HOUSE
Westport, Connecticut • London

Library of Congress Cataloging-in-Publication Data

Old and homeless—double-jeopardy : an overview of current practice and policies / edited by Diane Wiatt Rich, Thomas A. Rich, and Larry C. Mullins.

p. cm.

Includes bibliographical references and index.

ISBN 0-86569-246-7 (alk. paper)

1. Homeless aged—Services for—United States. 2. Homeless aged—Health and hygiene—United States. I. Rich, Diane Wiatt. II. Rich, Thomas A. III. Mullins, Larry C.

HV4504.043 1995

362.6'08'6942—dc20 94-36223

British Library Cataloguing in Publication Data is available.

Library of Congress Catalog Card Number: 94-36223
ISBN: 0-86569-246-7

First published in 1995

Auburn House, 88 Post Road West, Westport, CT 06881
An imprint of Greenwood Publishing Group, Inc.

Printed in the United States of America

The paper used in this book complies with the Permanent Paper Standard issued by the National Information Standards Organization (Z39.48-1984).

10 9 8 7 6 5 4 3 2 1

Copyright Acknowledgments

Frontispiece by William Cotter.
Photographs by James R. Roorda and Irena M. Zuk.

Admiration and affection are expressed to Kathryn Snoddy Martinez, who has been dedicated to the success of this project from the time it was merely an idea through its completion in 1994. We would like to express our appreciation to the Hillsborough County Coalition for the Homeless and the Pinellas County Homeless Coalition for their valuable assistance in collecting the data for the Tampa Bay Survey of Older Homeless Adults. We especially valued our interactions with the older homeless adults, without whom this work could not have been accomplished. Finally, we would like to give recognition to the Retirement Research Foundation for its vision and support of the Older Homeless Adult Project.

Editors

Contents

Foreword ix
Harold L. Sheppard

Introduction xi
Diane Wiatt Rich and Thomas A. Rich

1. Labels and Social Context 1
Diane Wiatt Rich

2. Double Jeopardy: Homeless and Old 7
James R. Roorda

3. Characteristics and Needs: Service and Policy Implications 11
Thomas A. Rich, Diane Wiatt Rich, and Louisette A. Boucher

4. Mental Health Overview 17
Irena M. Zuk

5. Mental Health: Recognition and Referral 23
Thomas A. Rich

6. Substance Abuse 29
Louisette A. Boucher

7. Physical Health Issues 47
Irena M. Zuk

8. Medication: Overview and Issues 53
Louisette A. Boucher

9. Psychotropic Medications 65
Louisette A. Boucher

10. Outreach and Empowerment 79
Judith Sullivan-Mintz

11. Community Resources 91
Judith Sullivan-Mintz

12. Housing Overview 101
Irena M. Zuk

13. Housing Policy 111
Larry C. Mullins

14. Concluding Thoughts 117
Diane Wiatt Rich and Thomas A. Rich

Appendix 119
Old and Homeless in Tampa Bay: A Survey
Thomas A. Rich, Louisette A. Boucher, and Diane Wiatt Rich

Index 139

About the Contributors 141

Foreword

Harold L. Sheppard

A major principle in the study of aging is the concept of *heterogeneity*. This volume is a dynamic testimony to that principle because it demonstrates, first, that there is no such phenomenon as *the* aged: The population of older adults contains a myriad of subgroups, not to mention a number of sub-*age* groups. Second, older homeless adults themselves are made up of several categories, a point which is amply described in this volume. They are not a homogeneous entity consisting, for example, only of mentally ill men and women. They are not a homogeneous entity consisting only of women who have become victims of divorces, leaving them impoverished in their middle-aged years or later. Other categories of older homeless adults have their portraits sketched herein.

Returning to the discussion of heterogeneity, Florida evokes an image in the public mind of the playgrounds for America's truly leisure class--namely, the senior citizen or "greedy geezer" segment of our society. A reading of *Old and Homeless* should set that distorted image straight. Economists of aging know of the vast range in income distribution of the 65+ population, of the fact that the range reveals one of the largest indexes of *inequality* in income distribution. The use of *median* incomes obscures that inequality. Compared to younger age groups, American older adults are subjected to the greatest gaps between the lowest and the highest of income recipients.

The reasons and the conditions for the emergence of an older homeless adult cohort during the past few decades are discussed in the pages that follow. While many of the homeless suffer problems of mental health, drug addiction, and physical health, we must not assume that these factors are the root cause of homelessness. And we must not ignore the impact of *exogenous* factors such as inadequate housing policies, economic and employment circumstances, and policies over which the individual has little, if any, control.

It was historian Arnold Toynbee, I believe, who proclaimed that a real test of the humanity and level of civilization of any society is the status of its citizens in their later years. In future decades, as we move into the twenty-first century, how shall our own society be judged and evaluated? I hope the dissemination of *Old and Homeless* will stimulate an effective redress (the setting right that which is morally wrong) of the plight of being old and homeless in America.

HAROLD L. SHEPPARD, PH.D.
Professor, Department of Gerontology
University of South Florida
Tampa, Florida

Dr. Sheppard served as Counselor on Aging to President Jimmy Carter and was Director of the International Exchange Center on Gerontology at the University of South Florida.

Introduction

Diane Wiatt Rich and Thomas A. Rich

Older adults represent a growing and largely unrecognized segment of the homeless population. Shelters and other homeless agencies have been inundated in recent years by homeless persons of all ages and backgrounds. The greatest pressure has come from young families, who are increasingly likely to become homeless and in need of shelter and services. With these pressures, it is not surprising that older homeless adults have remained a somewhat unrecognized and under studied group.

The Retirement Research Foundation recognized the importance of meeting the needs of older homeless adults 50+. In 1991, it funded the Department of Aging and Mental Health, the Center for Applied Gerontology, and the Department of Gerontology of the University of South Florida to develop, test, and evaluate a national model training program for those working with older homeless adults. The Older Homeless Adult Project was initiated in collaboration with the Hillsborough County Coalition for the Homeless and the Pinellas County Homeless Coalition.

Florida served as an excellent laboratory for the project because it is an age concentrated state with a continuing population explosion and an economic recession. By using the Tampa Bay Area as the geographic and population area for the development of teaching materials, a broad heterogeneous population of older homeless adults aged 50+ was available for study in the context of a network of services seeking to assist the growing population of homeless in general. The Older Homeless Adult Project has addressed the combined problems of individuals facing the dual problems of aging and homelessness.

This book represents an interweaving of knowledge about aging and homelessness, and it was developed to be useful in undergraduate and graduate courses in disciplines such as gerontology, social work, rehabilitation counseling, social policy, and nursing. The materials could be used in workshops and in-service training for staff of aging services and staff/volunteers of agencies serving the homeless. Policy makers and administrators will also find the materials useful.

OLD AND HOMELESS — DOUBLE-JEOPARDY

1

Labels and Social Context

Diane Wiatt Rich

Little attention has been given to the history of homelessness in the Western world, yet our present attitudes and social policies in regard to homelessness are rooted in this history. With the current media attention to homelessness, one might have the impression that it is a new phenomenon. Homelessness has been a fact of life throughout history, though the labels given to the homeless have varied and in themselves reflect our attitudes. The basis for our current attitudes is of great import in the social policies we forge as well as in how we as individuals provide services.

Labels historically used to describe homeless individuals include such terms as *vagabonds*, *tramps*, *gypsies*, and *beggars* (beggars came to be categorized as deserving or undeserving). More recent terms to describe those who are homeless include *street people*, *hobos*, *bag ladies*, *bums*, and *winos*. The homeless have included those who were licensed to beg, such as university scholars and members of religious orders, as well as those who were defined as criminal because they were unemployed and maintained no permanent residence.

The term *homeless* encompasses a number of pejorative meanings rather than the description of merely being without a home. There is considerable ambiguity in the definition of *homeless*. At its core, *homelessness* means not having customary and regular access to a conventional dwelling (Rossi, 1989). There are, however, shades of homelessness, the definition of which can include those who are, as Rossi defines the problem, "precariously housed" (1989). However homelessness is defined, it is an "extreme manifestation of poverty and residential instability" (Bassuk & Buckner, 1992, p. 330).

History has seen many variants of this problem in all its shades of meaning for all age groups. Associated as it is with impoverishment, disability, unemployment, natural disaster, illness, and war, homelessness may indeed be endemic to human society (Caton, 1990). That we are still experiencing the problem suggests that our social policies are ineffective. Certainly our social policies are affected by society's attitudes toward those who are homeless and those who are older. Our individual and societal attitudes toward this disenfranchised, vulnerable group continue to be an issue of much concern.

HISTORICAL PERSPECTIVES

The treatment of the earliest wanderers was affected by attitudes based in a culture in which individuals generally stayed in blood-related groups. Attitudes and treatment directed toward those who wandered were tinged by mystery and folklore, as well as cultural mores which allowed any "guest" hospitality for a brief time. The dignity of those who wandered was further protected by religious philosophy which sanctified charity and provided relief to those in need. However, as the numbers without permanent residence increased, it became necessary to develop social policies. These early efforts were rooted in divisions of people into categories--those deserving of help and those considered undeserving.

In 1388, English law required that all persons moving from place to place (e.g., the destitute, laborers, university scholars, and members of religious orders) obtain letters from town officials authorizing travel. Failure to do so was punishable (Caton, 1990). Such laws also existed on the European continent, where groups such as university students or the disabled received licenses to beg. These fine distinctions of who was "allowed" to be poor and beg without being criminal resulted from laws passed during the Protestant Reformation. The Protestant Reformation was a period which saw a rise in the belief that work was a religious duty and which saw the failure to succeed as a signal that one had not worked hard enough or was looked on with disfavor by God. It was made illegal both to beg and to give alms (Cohen & Sokolovsky, 1989). These distinctions among those who could be licensed to beg led to occasional pretense in order to belong to a licensable group. Such fakery, described by Martin Luther in the *Book of Vagabonds and Beggars* created further negative attitudes toward those without homes.

Those in society found guilty of giving money or shelter to unlicensed beggars were themselves fined or imprisoned. Harsher punishments were meted out to the wanderers--branding, ear lopping, enslavement, execution, or deportation. Indeed, some English "homeless" were deported to the American colonies as criminals.

Punitive measures in Europe and England were ameliorated with laws such as the Poor Law Act of 1601 in England, which provided for taxation to assist the needy and the provision of work for the able bodied. Those who refused to work were jailed or deported (Caton, 1990). As the American colonies inherited some of England's "unworthy" poor, they also assumed a number of attitudes as well as the English model of care, which placed dependents in the hands of local communities. Under Elizabethan Poor Law, which influenced colonial New England, each town assumed responsibility for its own poor (Rossi, 1989). This care tended to be provided only to those poor who were settled members of the community. Nonmembers with adequate means might petition to become town members; those without such means, including the elderly and disabled, became transient poor. Such settlement issues in the United States continued into the 1960s (Rossi, 1989).

Institutions for the provision of shelter for the homeless appeared in the United States in the early eighteenth century. One of the first was the "Poor House, Work House, and House of Correction of New York City" (Caton, 1990). The mentally ill, but able bodied, were also served in the same settings. Such a combination of poorhouse/jail reflects the prevailing attitudes toward poverty, unemployment, and criminality associated with such settings.

Despite the growing numbers of services, the problems of homelessness continued. Increasing numbers of homeless were housed in police stations, eventually leading to the establishment of almshouses as residences for those without homes. By the mid-nineteenth century, approximately 10,000 homeless, a quarter of whom were children, were housed in this manner (Caton, 1990).

BURGEONING NUMBERS

Following the American Civil War, numbers of people became displaced throughout the United States. Those affected included veterans of both sides of the conflict living in an economy ruined by war, especially in the area of agriculture. These numbers were increased by particularly massive post-Civil War immigration.

Debate continued over worthy and unworthy poor, and states passed statutes concerning tramps, who were considered to be able bodied, lazy, and unemployed (Keyssar, 1991). In opposition to the view that being unemployed was a form of criminal behavior, the then governor of Kansas attacked the Kansas vagrancy statute of 1889, stating that the debate over worthiness and poverty was academic, that being unemployed should not be a crime, and that such statutes assume job availability (Caton, 1990).

As unemployment rose during the post-Civil War era (to between 30 and 40 percent in 1873), skid row areas spread from origins in the logging areas of Washington State to other parts of the United States. These streets, lined with flophouses, bars, and brothels, provided social support for those on the move looking for employment. With no concerted national policy, relief was provided by such organizations as the Salvation Army and the YMCA.

The number of homeless fluctuated in the late nineteenth and early twentieth centuries. In the early decades of the twentieth century, there was an increase in migrant workers using Chicago as the focal point for labor exchange. This image of the hobo has been romanticized as a life of adventure--a view played out in many stories and pieces of music, such as Roger Miller's "King of the Road" (Pals, 1992). The Depression-era homeless, of course, have been well documented in film, music, and literature.

World War II saw the passage of statutes which were aimed at preventing the displacement and homelessness which so frequently has followed the disruption caused by war. Such measures included the G.I. Bill and other veterans' benefit programs. Vietnam veterans, by some accounts, have not fared so well and seem to be overrepresented in the current homeless population. According to Veterans Administration estimates, approximately 30 percent of the homeless population are veterans, most of whom are middle-aged males who are unemployed or underemployed (Levine, 1984). These numbers will add to the numbers of homeless aged 50+ in the near future.

We currently have an increasing number of homeless individuals and those at risk for homelessness (i.e., those without conventional, permanent housing). Among these homeless are rising numbers of children, families, working poor, and an often invisible population of older adults.

OLDER HOMELESS ADULTS

The numbers of homeless are difficult to count and estimate. This is especially true for subgroups, such as the older homeless, and those who are precariously housed. The reality is that the percentage of older adults in the United States is growing and among them are adults who have grown old on the street, adults who are recently homeless, and those who are at risk for homelessness. According to Kutza and Keigher (1991), the demographics of the group suggest that their numbers will continue to grow, while their options for reintegration into society are few.

While those 62+ more likely have a steady income, primarily from Social Security, these benefits are often too low to cover housing costs. Those between 50 and 62 fall through the cracks and are not yet eligible for Social Security and Medicare, although their physical health is more like that of a 70-year-old. Additionally, older homeless adults have a multitude of health problems, which increase their vulnerability. Further, older adults are at increased risk of losing their homes and are unable to function well in the streets along with the younger homeless (Doolin, 1985). Kutza and Keigher (1991) assert that the elderly, particularly the female elderly, are emerging as the newest group caught in homelessness because of economic and social problems. It is clear that many young and middle-aged homeless people will age into homelessness as well.

REFERENCES

Bassuk, E. L., & Buckner, J. C. (1992). Out of mind--out of sight. *American Journal of Orthopsychiatry*, *62*(3), 330-331.

Caton, C. L. M. (1990). *Homeless in America*. New York: Oxford University Press.

Cohen, C. I., & Sokolovsky, J. (1989). *Old men of the Bowery: Strategies for survival among the homeless*. New York: The Guilford Press.

Doolin, J. (1985, March/April). "America's untouchables, the elderly homeless." *Perspective on Aging*, pp. 8-11. Cited in *The new homeless crisis: Old and poor in the streets*. Hearing before the Select Committee on Aging, House of Representatives, Committee No. 101-784, September 26, 1990 (pp. 96-99). Washington, DC.

Keyssar, A. (1991). Introduction. *Social Research*. *58*(1), 87-91.

Kutza, E. A., & Keigher, S. M. (1991). The elderly "new homeless": An emerging population at risk. *Social Work*, *36*(4), 278-293.

Levine, I. S. (1984). Homelessness: Its implications for mental health policy and practice. *Psychosocial Rehabilitation Journal*, *VIII*(1), 6-15.

"Pals, hobos mourn singer, Roger Miller." (1992, October 27). *St. Petersburg Times*, p. 7b.

Rossi, P. H. (1989). *Down and out in America: The origins of homelessness*. Chicago: The University of Chicago Press.

2

Double Jeopardy: Homeless and Old

James R. Roorda

Numerous studies have been conducted on the effects of stereotyping by age (ageism). There is also information concerning the stereotyping of the homeless population. The purpose here is threefold: (1) to define ageism and discuss its impact; (2) to discuss homeless stereotypes; and (3) to examine the impact of stereotypes of age and homelessness.

AGE STEREOTYPES

Ageism is a term probably first used by Robert N. Butler (1975) in his book *Why Survive? Being Old in America.* It is a term that describes patterns of widely held attitudes and stereotypes about aging and older adults and a term that devalues the target population (Gatz & Pearson, 1988). Ageism is no more a benign holding of attitude than racism and sexism are. Stereotypes are distortions of fact, negative and exaggerated, overgeneralizing the characteristics of an entire group.

Arluke and Levin (1984) offer the most descriptive definition of ageism and its effects when they describe stereotypes as "culturally shared and institutionalized negative images which are used to justify unequal treatment, or discrimination, directed toward minority groups, ranging from perpetrating petty indignities in everyday life to slavery and genocide" (p. 7).

HOMELESS STEREOTYPES

Do stereotypes of older adults influence perceptions of older homeless people? Stereotyping of the homeless has not been given its own distinctive term. Nevertheless, the damage and barriers that result are as harmful to this population as to any group. When a group is viewed through distortions it becomes easier to ignore its members and their special problems. It may become particularly easy to ignore problems that society feels unable to address, especially what we fear most--poor health and dependency (Briggs, 1987). The older homeless adult frequently represents both poor health and dependence.

What is perceived about older homeless adults may be a mixture of both truth and myth. The Michigan Department of Mental Health (Mowbray, Johnson, Solare, & Combs, 1984) conducted a research study of homelessness in Detroit and reported consistent results from several sources. The data come from multiple sites, such as soup kitchens, emergency shelters, and a psychiatric hospital. The study concludes that many commonly held stereotypes of the homeless are not accurate. These inaccuracies include beliefs that most homeless people are old, male, without recent work, transient, former mental patients, career homeless, and homeless by choice. Some characteristics which do seem representative are (1) numerous health problems, (2) high alcohol use, (3) more psychiatric symptoms, (4) marginal education and work skills, and (5) lack of social supports.

ORIGINS OF STEREOTYPES

Our views of life are determined largely by the culture in which we are raised. We learn attitudes and values; we also learn myths and stereotypes. Most of us acquire both positive and negative attitudes about older adults from familial relationships, such as grandparents. Our personal view of our grandparents, for example, may be more positive than our view of the older neighbor down the street. Through the rationalization process we can develop aging stereotypes, seeing other older adults as the exception. We are simultaneously able to hold contradictory views. Those views are also formed in ways other than personal experience.

Television and other media have played a large part in forming the values and attitudes of people. Bishop and Krause (1984) conclude that, although it is not a major theme in television programming, the topic of age emerges in negative images which reinforce dominant cultural stereotypes about aging in our society. In their study of Saturday morning cartooning, being old is seen as "not healthy, not attractive, and not good" (p. 93). While we begin to see some positive older role models in television today, negative images continue. Cartooning, in particular, exaggerates and accentuates the physical features of characters in order to identify their roles. Stereotyping is virtually synonymous with cartooning. Children's cartoons are not subtle; heroes look like heroes, young characters look young, and old characters look old.

OLDER HOMELESS ADULTS

Homelessness precludes a single characterization. Although some studies characterize the typical homeless person as male, young, and single, recent evidence reveals larger populations of people with special needs, including older adults and families with children. Older homeless adults are a small but growing vulnerable subpopulation that needs special attention. As Kutza and Keigher (1991) have indicated, "their age alone renders this group particularly vulnerable. Their options for reintegrating into the dominant social and economic structure of society are few. Their physical capacity to withstand living on the streets or in shelters is limited" (p. 288). Their plight is exacerbated by stereotypes of age.

SUMMARY

It is clear that the demographics of homelessness will change because, whatever the character of homelessness, it is a population that is aging with the rest of society. It is difficult to find literature specifically addressing older homeless adults and the effects of stereotypes and prejudices, but it appears that the burden for them is cumulative.

REFERENCES

Arluke, A., & Levin, J. (1984). Another stereotype: Old age as a second childhood. *Aging, 346*, 7-11.

Bishop, J. M., & Krause, D. R. (1984). Depictions of aging and old age on Saturday morning television. *The Gerontologist*, 24(1), 91-94.

Briggs, H. (1987). Images of aging. In H. Briggs (Ed.), *Teaching aging*. (pp. 1-40). Tampa, FL: University of South Florida, Center for Applied Gerontology.

Butler, Robert N. (1975). Why survive? Being old in America. New York: Harper & Row.

Gatz, M., & Pearson, C. G. (1988). Ageism revised and the provision of psychological services. *American Psychologist*, *43*(3), 184-188.

Kutza, E. A., & Keigher, S. M. (1991). The elderly "new homeless": An emerging population at risk. *Social Work*, *36*(4), 288-293.

Mowbray, C. T., Johnson, S. V., Solare, A., & Combs, C. J. (1984). *Mental Health and Homeless in Detroit: A Research Study* (NIMH Grant #5H84-MH-#5823-04SL). Detroit, MI: Michigan Department of Mental Health.

3

Characteristics and Needs: Service and Policy Implications

Thomas A. Rich, Diane Wiatt Rich, and Louisette A. Boucher

The homeless population has increased across the United States, straining the human service system as well as becoming a major policy issue. While homelessness is a condition recognized historically for centuries, the numbers of homeless are increasing in the United States as well as in the rest of the world. Many factors have contributed to this growth, including the deinstitutionalization movement in the 1960s, the decrease in priority for low cost housing funding in the 1980s, and the economic downturn of the early 1990s with the diminished availability of unskilled and low-tech jobs. The major growth of the homeless population has been in the numbers of young families with children, who for these and a variety of reasons find themselves temporarily without the resources necessary to maintain independent living. Therefore, they must seek help in shelters and other agencies.

Florida has long been recognized for its concentration of older adults and the special needs and demands of this growing population. Only recently has this relationship between an age-concentrated population and older homeless adults been noted. This group has been generally invisible, with little special attention given to its specific needs. The Retirement Research Foundation in Chicago has funded three national projects on older homeless adults, including one at the University of South Florida.

To provide a better perspective on the characteristics and needs of older homeless adults, a survey was conducted in Florida's Hillsborough and Pinellas counties in 1991 to develop a profile of older homeless adults in these counties (see the Appendix). A sample of 103 adults over age 50 were interviewed, about half of whom were living in shelters and about half of whom were living in other locations, including parks, woods, abandoned houses, and vans. While a few older adults report that they like to be on the street, the majority express a preference for stable housing and better care settings than they presently experience.

The older homeless adults reported the same physical problems found in the general population of older adults and a similar need for care of chronic conditions. This need contrasts with the fact that service provided tends to be the more expensive emergency care for acute problems. A major health problem reported by half the subjects was the need for dental care.

Some older homeless represent the results of deinstitutionalization and have a history of mental problems. Others experience symptoms associated with depression and anxiety. Some of those interviewed have major problems with alcohol and/or drugs, and some use alcohol for self-medication.

As a gerontologist looking at this brief description, it appears that older homeless adults have many problems in common with the general population of low-income older adults. The difference between them is that for a variety of reasons, such as divorce and loss of job, individuals are unable to maintain themselves in independent housing and have become dependent for survival on the variety of homeless agencies.

For the purpose of the Tampa Bay survey, older homeless adults were defined as age 50+, the accepted age in the research literature. Defining *older* as 50+ describes well those living on the street, as they tend to age prematurely. Many programs intended to serve older adults are not available to those in their early 50s, and some programs are available at age 55, 60, 62, or 65. This patchwork of age requirements for service complicates the existence of these people. A further problem is that some homeless are unaware of benefits and entitlements for which they are eligible; still others need assistance in negotiating the complexities of the application process. The Tampa Bay survey indicates that few of the respondents are collecting benefits.

Aging service agencies have begun to recognize the older homeless as a problem population in need of identification and assistance. The overworked homeless coalitions have also just begun to recognize that they have an older population which may be far larger than earlier estimates indicated and that this is one more demand on their services. Bringing older homeless adults into the mainstream of services available to all older adults may be one of the issues that needs further consideration.

There is a continuing age-related shift in terms of health and physical problems for survival on the streets. The age of eligibility for services for older adults through the Older Americans Act as well as the increased availability of pensions, Social Security, and other benefits for the older age group also separates the group. With further consideration, policy issues and services provision should address the group 50-59 as a separate segment of the older adult population and the population 60+ as a group targeted for increased emphasis as older adults, and not just as homeless. This would follow the trend in age-related policy and service to address the population of older adults 75+ as a group separate from the group 60+ in terms of their needs and characteristics.

There is a need to begin to address the issues of homelessness for service and policy beyond the nuisance level of rules and regulations, such as whether the homeless should be allowed to sleep anywhere; whether arm rests should be placed on park benches, making it impossible to sleep there; and whether parts of cities should be designated as places where homeless may sleep, rest, or camp. For the most part, older homeless adults would prefer to be off the streets and would best be served by having housing and supports that meet their needs for independence and self-respect.

Current policy directions, nationally and locally, tend to hold promise for a move in the direction of an optimum continuum of care that leads individuals out of homelessness. The Clinton Administration, through the Department of Housing and Urban Development (HUD), offers promise of a new national perspective on homelessness and has taken steps to address homelessness not just as a matter of provision of shelter but as needing a comprehensive system of services, in addition to permanent housing. This system and philosophy strives to fulfill those requirements with three fundamental components: emergency shelter, transitional housing with social services, and permanent housing. More importantly, this approach recognizes that the homeless needs in each community, as well as current resources and systems to meet those needs, are as different and distinct as the people who live in these communities (U. S., 1994).

A national perspective with such an underlying philosophy permits individual communities to design strategies which work best. Among these is the ability to provide services to the homeless that may be age appropriate in those communities where there are large numbers of older adults and, likely, a larger proportion of older homeless adults among the homeless population. Such communities generally have more services designed specifically for older adults and hence the possibility of cooperative effort between the homeless and aging service providers.

HUD's new approach to homeless problems changes the situation that has existed whereby there has been little strategic planning and no clear assessment of the needs of the homeless population within the existing community structure (U. S., 1994). This approach encourages a streamlined process that enables communities to develop coordinated, comprehensive approaches to meet the needs of local homeless populations. This promotes an effective system with needed components in a continuum of care approach. Further, this effort would encourage partnerships with homeless providers, state and local governments, and nonprofit agencies which would work particularly well toward developing partnerships with aging service agencies and homeless agencies attempting to serve older homeless adults and those at risk for homelessness.

The Hillsborough County Coalition for the Homeless (1994) has proposed a further expansion of such a concept by suggesting the following as the ideal service continuum for the homeless and specifically addressing the unique needs of older homeless adults. These services are (1) services for older homeless adults for their unique needs; (2) prevention services, including education services for those at risk and for preventing recurrence; (3) improvement of referral services; (4) employment assistance; (5) improvement of data collection; (6) assistance in obtaining benefits and entitlements; (7) case management; and (8) staff training to bridge the gap between aging and homelessness among homeless and aging network agencies.

An example of such integration can be seen in the recent ACCESS grants to nine states (National Resource Center, 1993). While these grants deal specifically with the integration of services for homeless persons with severe mental illnesses, they could provide a prototype of service integration between aging services and homeless services. The ACCESS program, recommended by the Federal Task Force on Homelessness and Severe Mental Illness, encourages all agencies providing services to homeless persons (government, local, and voluntary) to eliminate the fragmentation that currently exists in the care-giving infrastructure. The central idea of ACCESS is the idea of *any-door access*. Any homeless person with a severe mental illness will be able to enter by any service door, be assessed, and obtain a full complement of services in an effort to make the outreach and service as barrier free as possible (National Resource Center, 1993). Such a model could clearly be of assistance in integrating aging services and homeless agencies for that group of homeless adults 60+.

Such innovative social policies and programs on a national and local level are needed to address the causes and effects of homelessness on individuals and communities. As Schutt and Garrett (1992) note, "it has become clear that homelessness is both cause and consequence of multiple systemic and personal difficulties, but ... through the creative application of effective policies and programs, the difficulties of homeless persons can be lessened and the prevalence of homelessness itself reduced" (p. 221).

REFERENCES

Hillsborough County Coalition for the Homeless. (1994). *Long Range Plan, 1994, Part I.* Tampa, FL: Hillsborough County.

National Resource Center on Homelessness and Mental Illness. (1993). ACCESS grantees test services integration strategies. *ACCESS: Information from the National Resource Center on Homelessness and Mental Illness*, *5*(4), 1 & 3. Delmar, NY: Policy Research Associates, Inc.

Schutt, R. K., & Garrett, G. R. (1992). *Responding to the homeless: Policy and practice*. New York: Plenum Press.

U. S. Department of Housing and Urban Development Office of Community Planning and Development. (1994, April). Continuum of care: A complete approach to meet homeless needs. *Community Connections*, pp. 1 & 3. Washington, DC: HUD.

4

Mental Health Overview

Irena M. Zuk

If older adults are not mentally ill before they find themselves without a home and on the streets, they may soon develop some form of psychological problem once there. Flynn (1985) reports that homelessness creates a feeling of powerlessness and of hopelessness. There is a sense of inadequacy and a loss of ability to control one's destiny. In spite of a growing understanding of the plight of the homeless, there is still much prejudice, even among professionals, against both the older adult and the homeless (Hudson, Rauch, Dawson, Santos, & Burdick, 1990).

Decisions determining lives and health care are made by government regulations, efficiency and availability of service agencies, and the ability to access aid. Unfortunately, according to O'Connell, Summerfield, and Kellogg (1990), some older adults choose the street when their only other options are nursing homes or chronic care hospitals. Others develop a sense of identity and self-esteem on the streets which they lost when they were rejected by their families.

When older adults are placed in shelters, which are often crowded and noisy, their condition may suffer a sharp decline, especially if they already have physical or mental problems and require supervision with medications (Mellinger, 1989). As great as their need is, older adults, out of fear, tend to stay away from shelters and clinics (Kellermann, Halper, Hopkins, Nayowith, 1985). Hudson et al. (1990) believe that when older adults finally do go for help, they are often too disoriented to follow directions for medications or future appointments. As we further investigate this situation, we will review the following aspects of mental illness among older homeless adults: history, causes, statistics, government programs, and innovative solutions.

HISTORY

Deinstitutionalization is frequently blamed for the great increase in the numbers of the mentally ill homeless. This contention, however, deserves further examination. During the 1960s, there was a movement to curtail involuntary commitment to mental hospitals. The move to eliminate some of these institutions came about with the intent of integrating the mentally ill into a more "normal" environment. Federally funded community mental health centers were established to replace closed state hospitals (*The Harvard Mental Health Letter*, July, 1990) but were insufficient in number to meet the needs of the mentally ill.

Under the Stewart B. McKinney Homeless Assistance Act of 1987, $35 million in grants was appropriated for fiscal year 1987 to provide outpatient mental health services for the chronically mentally ill. The controversy over deinstitutionalization persists. Breakey (1989) and Levin and Stockdill (1984) insist that the major cause of homelessness among the mentally ill is not deinstitutionalization, but others disagree.

CAUSES AND STATISTICS

The mentally ill do not find themselves on the streets as a result of one crisis, but rather as a result of problems which may have begun earlier. Approximately one half have been in foster care as children or were hospitalized for mental health problems (*The Harvard Mental Health Letter*, July, 1990). It is difficult to tell which of the many events is the prime cause of homelessness. It could be loss of housing, family estrangement, cutbacks in benefits, a psychotic episode, or worsening of drug or alcohol dependency (Mauch & Mulkern, 1991). Economic recession in conjunction with diminishing state resources and increasing unemployment foreshadows increased numbers of mentally ill homeless.

Levin and Stockdill (1984) believe that factors which contribute to homelessness are unemployment, cutbacks in the Social Security system and complexities involved in accessing assistance, diminished low-cost housing, urban renewal, and family disintegration. These authors feel that these factors especially affect the mentally ill because they are placed at the lower end of societal status. HUD reinforces the idea that homelessness is not caused merely by a lack of shelter, but involves a variety of underlying unmet needs. *The Harvard Mental Health Letter* (July, 1990) points out that the disabilities of the very poor make it exceptionally difficult for family and friends to deal with financial, physical, and mental dependencies. Rents grow beyond means and the mentally ill and alcoholics can find themselves on the streets. Few indicate that they have friends or family they can count on. Once on the street, broken ties are virtually impossible to mend, and the new homeless become the permanent homeless.

According to Burt (1992), studies show that between 25 and 30 percent of the homeless suffer from severe mental health problems, yet only four percent receive Supplemental Security Income (SSI) benefits. They may have lost their eligibility or never have been in touch with an agency that could help them with the complicated application process. The Social Security Administration has attempted to assist those with mental health problems in accessing the SSI system through such projects as a Florida grant, Linking Supplemental Security Income with Community Mental Health (Rich, 1992).

Not only do 62 percent of the mentally ill have more than one barrier to overcome when seeking employment in comparison to those without this handicap, once they land a job, they are less successful in keeping it (Tessler & Dennis, 1989). In spite of a high level of disability, fewer than one third surveyed in New York City, Boston, and Milwaukee receive public benefits. This contributes to becoming and remaining *long-term homeless* (Tessler & Dennis, 1989). In addition to psychiatric problems, the mentally ill homeless also have poorer health and receive less treatment for physical maladies than do the homeless without a mental illness. Drug and alcohol abuse contribute greatly to their poor health (Tessler & Dennis, 1989). Should they be dually diagnosed, they may not be accepted into alcohol detoxification programs.

Tessler and Dennis (1989) stress the importance of determining why the mentally ill homeless reject psychiatric services and how these can be made more acceptable. *The Harvard Mental Health Letter* (August, 1990) indicates that the mental health system does not serve the needs of the homeless and reports that the homeless older adult is overwhelmed by the complexity of the system.

GOVERNMENT PROGRAMS

In 1987, the Stewart B. McKinney Homeless Assistance Act and the Mental Health Services for the Homeless (MHSH) block grant program were passed to support state coordination of services to the homeless mentally ill (Mauch & Mulkern, 1991). These services included "outreach; community mental health services; medical and psychiatric referrals; case management; and supportive services in residential settings" (Mauch & Mulkern, 1991, p. 2). When states evaluated the programs, they found a high success rate in housing stability, a decrease in hospitalization, more efficient use of crisis services, and integration into the mental health service system. Of the number of homeless mentally ill surveyed, 101,972 were served by the

MHSH program. Older homeless adults were overlooked, and the majority of those served were under the age of 45.

Jones (1990) describes a collaborative agreement between the Department of Health and Human Services and HUD. There are three interdepartmental workgroups which develop coordinated health and housing initiatives for homeless families with children, families on welfare, and homeless individuals with severe mental illness. These groups are considered most vulnerable and most at risk of becoming homeless. The HUD staff has held training sessions on how to review housing program grant proposals and mental health service components of these grants. Special preference is given to those who submit a housing proposal to HUD and a research application to the National Institute of Mental Health (NIMH). For eligibility, the research projects should include "comprehensive mental health services that are coordinated with housing" (Jones, 1990, p. 19).

The Committee on Health Care for Homeless People (Institute of Medicine, 1988) reports that the long commitment by the government to provide specialized housing, as under the Community Mental Health Centers Act of 1962, has never been followed through on federal or state levels. Although the Emergency Assistance Program was established to provide subsidized housing, it should be restructured not merely to alleviate homelessness but to prevent it. Blanch, Carling, and Ridgway (1988) feel that the government pattern may be changing, with $367 million having been allocated to 46 states in response to the need for residential programs to serve the mentally ill homeless (Blanch et al., 1988). In 1988, the preliminary data counted over 3,000 residential programs and facilities in operation across the country. Blanch et al. (1988) feel that the highest priority services have become independent living, housing supports, and case management (37 percent) with semi-independent living (29 percent). Community support and membership in coalitions to lobby for public funds and policy are still of utmost importance.

INNOVATIVE SOLUTIONS

Kellermann et al. (1985) believe that what is needed to serve mentally ill older adults is long-term transitional housing. Such housing can provide supervision and follow-up care. Board and care homes with social activities are especially beneficial. Unfortunately, those housing arrangements which would most benefit the homeless mentally ill are poorly funded. Flynn (1985), and Mauch and Mulkern (1991) agree that a more viable solution to the immediacy of older homeless adult problems is needed. They suggest an outreach program, possibly employing former homeless older adults, to seek out those in need.

It is also important to evaluate family relationships and social networking as part of the mental health treatment of the homeless (Tessler & Dennis, 1989; Toro & Wall, 1991). If such ties cannot be rekindled, it is important for the client to have a relationship with a therapist or other professional.

SUMMARY

The leveling effect of homelessness is remarkable. Those with and without mental illness are reported in only slightly different terms (Tessler & Dennis, 1989). It becomes apparent that what is needed to better serve the mentally ill homeless, especially the older adult, is comprehensive case management. Such case management would provide treatment and services specific to the mental health problems of the older homeless adult.

REFERENCES

Blanch, A. K., Carling, P. J., & Ridgway, P. (1988). Normal housing with specialized supports: A psychiatric rehabilitation approach to living in the community. *Rehabilitation Psychology, 33*(1), 47-55.

Breakey, W. (1989). Mental health of the homeless. *The Harvard Medical School Mental Health Letter, 6*(9), 5-6.

Burt, Martha R. (1992). *Over the edge: The growth of homelessness in the 1980s.* Washington, DC: The Urban Institute Press.

Flynn, K. (1985). The toll of deinstitutionalization. In P. W. Brickner, L. K. Scharer, B. Conanan, B., A. Elvy, & M. Savarese (Eds.), *Health care of homeless people* (pp. 189-204). New York: Springer-Verlag.

The Harvard Mental Health Letter. (1990). Mental illness and homelessness: Part I. *The Harvard Mental Health Letter, 7*(1), 1-4.

The Harvard Mental Health Letter. (1990). Mental illness and homelessness: Part II. *The Harvard Mental Health Letter, 7*(2), 1-4.

Hudson, B. A., Rauch, B. B., Dawson, G. D., Santos, J. F., & Burdick, D.C. (1990). *Homelessness: Special problems related to training, research, and the elderly.* Unpublished paper. University of Notre Dame, Department of Psychology, South Bend, IN.

Institute of Medicine, Committee on Health Care for Homeless People. (1988). *Homelessness, health, and human needs.* Washington, DC: National Academy Press.

Jones, P. (1990). Mental health and housing join to help homeless mentally ill. *ADAMHA News, XVI*(4), 18-19.

Kellermann, S. L., Halper, R. S., Hopkins, M., & Nayowith, G. B. (1985). Psychiatry and homelessness: Problems and programs. In P.W.

Brickner, L. K. Scharer, B. Conanan, A. Elvy, & M. Savarese (Eds.), *Health care of homeless people* (pp. 179-188). New York: Springer-Verlag.

Levin, I. S., & Stockdill, J. W. (1984). Mentally ill and homeless: A national problem. In B. E. Jones (Ed.), *Treating the homeless: Urban psychiatry's challenge* (pp. 1-16). Washington, DC: American Psychiatric Press, Inc.

Mauch, D., & Mulkern, V. (1991). *The McKinney mental health services for the homeless block grant program: A summary of FY 1989 annual reports*. Prepared for the National Institute of Mental Health, Office of Programs for the Homeless Mentally Ill.

Mellinger, J. C. (1989). Emergency housing for frail older adults. *The Gerontologist*, *29*(3), 401-405.

O'Connell, J. J., Summerfield, J., & Kellogg, F. R. (1990). The homeless elderly. In P. W. Brickner, L. K. Scharer, B. A. Conanan, M. Savarese, & B. C. Scanlan (Eds.), *Under the safety net* (pp. 151-168). New York: Springer-Verlag.

Rich, D. W. (Ed.). (1992). *Linking Supplemental Security Income with community mental health*. Tampa, FL: University of South Florida.

Tessler, R. C., & Dennis, D. L. (1989). *A synthesis of NIMH-funded research concerning persons who are homeless and mentally ill*. Program for the Homeless Mentally Ill. Division of Education and Service Systems Liaison. Bethesda, MD: National Institute of Mental Health Institute Press.

Toro, P. A., & Wall, D. D. (1991). Research on homeless persons: Diagnostic comparisons and practice implications. *Professional Psychology: Research and Practice*, *22*(6), 479-488.

5

Mental Health: Recognition and Referral

Thomas A. Rich

Older adults suffer from the same emotional and psychological problems that younger adults experience, though there are important differences in how they are presented. Depression may be shown through inactivity and in other passive ways and therefore may not be easily diagnosed. Older adults are more likely to suffer from dementia or delirium because those conditions increase with age. There is debate about the likelihood of schizophrenia appearing in older adults; there may be continuing schizophrenic processes that have been with a person throughout life. More important than these problems may be our failure to look consistently at older adults as people in need of counseling for such problems as anxiety or marital difficulties. These problems may be compounded by illness, loneliness, and loss of spouse and friends.

Most people have some emotional crises in their lives, and this is true of older adults. The important issue for staff or caretaker is not the diagnosis but rather the recognition that something is troubling the older adult. When older adults become dysfunctional in the ability to relate, to communicate, to work, or when they withdraw, their life is disrupted and they will need special assistance. Many individuals have strange diets, sleeping problems, feelings of uselessness, odd thoughts, and overreactions to body symptoms. Others fear crossing a bridge, flying, being in crowded rooms or open spaces, or going up a ramp to an interstate. Others are too neat, too messy, or feel that someone is out to get them. It would be unusual for any given person not to have felt some of these things during life. Again, if these things dominate one's behavior and the person is no longer able to function, it becomes a problem in need of intervention.

Older homeless adults suffer from all these problems. These are compounded by such things as fear and stress caused by having limited resources, being on the streets where safety is a major consideration, having limited access to medical or psychological assistance, and not knowing where the next meal is coming from. Many older homeless adults appear to try to treat themselves through alcohol abuse and to a lesser extent the use of drugs. While alcohol use is found in all age groups, a much higher percentage of homeless persons abuse alcohol or drink excessively. Alcoholism must be treated as a major mental health problem of older adults.

There are several major problems from which older adults and older homeless adults may suffer. The first is depression. Severe depression is perhaps not found any more frequently than in other age groups, but various levels of depression are found and are particularly damaging to older adults. If one is around an older adult who expresses feelings of sadness, pessimism, guilt, worthlessness, and loss of interest; is oversleeping or undersleeping; experiences weight loss or gain and fatigue; thinks about death, is irritable, has difficulty remembering things or making decisions; and has frequent headaches and digestion and chronic pain problems, then one is probably seeing someone who is depressed. With an older person, depression is particularly critical because of the inactivity which may occur. Older people are more likely to lose functional ability, to have problems with nutrition, and to overmedicate. These conditions must be recognized, and depressed older adults must be reassured that they can improve with professional assistance and must not merely be told to "snap out of it." They need professional diagnosis and determination of the most appropriate treatment for their condition.

Anxiety is also a common problem of older adults. As they lose control of life choices and survive on the street with few resources, anxiety can become a major problem. In institutional settings, including shelters, there is little choice about food, mealtime and bedtime. Anxiety should be recognized and treated. Anxiety may turn to apathy, a condition of learned helplessness. If nothing one does changes anything in life, one may stop trying, as has been noted in research in mental hospital patients. This can occur in almost all care or living settings and even at home, where overcare may reduce the responsibility and the freedom of the individual to make decisions. Individuals may go from anxiety to apathy and may have responses similar to depression.

Dementia is the most frequently discussed problem of older adults, and particularly in recent years, Alzheimer's disease has been on center stage. When symptoms of memory loss and confusion are observed, it becomes important to seek differential diagnosis. The symptoms of dementia, particularly early dementia, can result from depression or from delirium (which has many causes, such as overmedication). The importance of early diagnosis is that delirium can often be treated and reversed, and the memory loss reversed. It is estimated that Alzheimer's occurs in about one out of 25 persons over 65, but this estimate becomes one out of four persons over 80 years of age. A thorough assessment is needed for diagnosis of dementia.

The cause of Alzheimer's is not yet understood. It is a disease of gradual onset, more common in females, and involves the aforementioned changes in memory and thinking as well as other self-care abilities. In addition to Alzheimer's, there are other common disorders that can lead to dementia such as multi-infarct, arteriosclerosis, atherosclerosis, and others. For many of these a known physical cause has been established.

ASSESSMENT

Recognition and referral for assessment is critical in response to the symptoms discussed thus far. All settings serving older adults--whether nursing homes, retirement homes, or homeless shelters--need staff who recognize these symptoms and are able to make appropriate referrals to agencies for assessment. A social, medical, psychological, psychiatric, and environmental assessment may be necessary to determine the real problem. For the homeless, special attention to nutritional status and medications is needed as well as consideration of the stress in their lifestyle.

There are significant barriers for older adults in receiving help, and particularly for older homeless adults. Some of these are as follows:

1. Caregivers/staff must recognize mental health problems so that early identification and referrals occur.
2. Older homeless adults have been virtually an invisible population, not recognized as having the problems that other older adults share. Calling this special group to the attention of agencies and relating their needs for assistance opens the door for diagnosis and treatment. Many are targeted for alcohol treatment, for example, because the alcoholic is more readily recognized. Other problems may not be identified as easily.
3. There is a lack of understanding and stigma about mental health problems. In a recent study, it was found that there is still a strong feeling that depression is a self-help disorder and that one should cure oneself. Resistance may come from the person needing help as well as from the person who should be making the referral (Rich & Rich, 1993).

The following reasons have been given consistently for why older adults, particularly those who are depressed, do not seek help (Rich & Rich, 1993):

1. They are fearful of being told that they have Alzheimer's disease or senility.
2. They are ashamed or embarrassed to talk.
3. They do not know where to go.

4. There is stigma attached to the possibility of being "crazy."
5. They believe that the problem is age, not depression.
6. They may be too impaired to help themselves.
7. They believe that there is something wrong with them and that they are not like anyone else, that the problems are unique.
8. They believe that professionals cannot help because they do not know how it feels.
9. Cost and/or fear of cost is a deterrent.

CAREGIVER/STAFF ISSUES

Caregivers and staff must be more sensitive to behaviors that suggest emotional problems. Both caregivers and older adults share many of the biases about mental health and mental illness which lead to underreferral and undertreatment. Caregivers also need referral or assistance in dealing with their own reactions to the daily stress of working with homeless adults.

SUGGESTED READING

Bachrach, L. (1992). What we know about homelessness among mentally ill persons: An analytical review and commentary. *Hospital and Community Psychiatry*, *43*(5), 453-464.

Cohen, C. I., Teresi, J., & Holmes, D. (1988). The mental health of old homeless men. *Journal of the American Geriatrics Society*, *36*, 492-501.

Courage, M., & Williams, D. (1986). An approach to the study of burnout in professional care providers in human service organizations. [Special issue: Burnout among social workers]. *Journal of Social Service Research*, *10*(1), 7-22.

Gillespie, D., & Numerof, R. (1991). Burnout among health service providers. *Administration and Policy in Mental Health*, *18*(3), 161-171.

Goerning, P., Wasylenki, D., & St. Onge, M. (1992). Gender differences among clients of a case management program. *Hospital and Community Psychiatry*, *43*(2), 160-165.

Grant, B., & Fowle, L. (1990). Standardized diagnostic interviews for alcohol research. *Alcohol Health and Research World*, *14*(4), 340-348.

Hall, L. (1991). Homelessness: A model for mental health intervention. *Administration and Policy in Mental Health*, *18*(6), 451-454.

Haus, A. (Ed.). (1988). *Working with homeless people: A guide for staff and volunteers*. New York: Columbia University Community Services.

Knight, Bob. (1986). *Psychotherapy with older adults*. Beverly Hills, CA: Sage.

Lewis, J., Lewis, M., & Souflee, F. (Eds.). (1991). *Management of human service programs* (2nd ed.). Pacific Grove, CA: Cole Publishing Company.

Lipowski, Z. (1989). Current concepts--geriatrics: Delirium in the elderly patient. *New England Journal of Medicine, 320*(9), 578-582.

Murphy, J., & Pardeck, J. (1986). The burnout syndrome and management style. *Clinical Supervisor, 4*(4), 35-44.

National Institute of Mental Health (1992). *Outcasts on Main Street: Report of the Federal Task Force on Homelessness and Severe Mental Illness* (Interagency Council on the Homeless, ADM 92-1904). Washington, DC: NIMH.

Neugarten, B. (1970). Adaptation and the life cycle. *Journal of Geriatric Psychiatry, 4*, 71-100.

Neugarten, B. (Ed.). (1972). *Middle age and aging: A reader in social psychology*. Chicago: The University of Chicago Press.

Penn, M., Romano, J., & Foat, D. (1988). The relationship between job satisfaction and burnout: A study of human service professionals. *Administration in Mental Health, 15*(3), 157-165.

Quinnett, P. (1989). *On becoming a health and human services manager*. New York: The Continuum Publishing Company.

Rich, T., & Rich, D. (1993, April). *Depression in older adults: A discussion of attitudes and barriers to treatment*. Paper presented at the Southern Gerontological Society 14th Annual Conference, Richmond, VA.

Struening, E., & Padgett, D. (1990). Physical health status, substance use and abuse, and mental disorders among homeless adults. *Journal of Social Issues, 46*(4), 65-81.

6

Substance Abuse

Louisette A. Boucher

Substance abuse involves mood-altering chemicals, whether ingested, inhaled, or given intravenously. Addiction is the habitual and compulsive use of legal drugs such as alcohol, prescribed drugs, or illegal drugs such as crack. One becomes addicted or dependent when one is unable to control the intake of the mood-altering substance (Hauss, 1988). Being a victim of the dependence is evidenced by increasing tolerance/usage; sneaking to obtain/use the chemical; and developing a lifestyle which revolves around the chemical. The person also begins to project self-hatred onto others, and health, emotional stability, and interpersonal relationships deteriorate. At that point, the mood-altering substance becomes a survival need instead of a search for euphoria (Kelly & Cousineau, 1990).

Alcohol/substance abuse is found in all parts of society, all races, both sexes, and at varying ages. The incidence in the general population is 11 to 15 percent for men and two to four percent for women (Institute of Medicine, 1988). A national study reported by Williams, Stenson, Parker, Harford, and Noble (1987) shows that 7.73 percent of males and 2.15 percent of females between 50 and 64 years of age are alcohol abusers and alcoholics as compared to 4.03 percent of males and 0.32 percent of females 65+. The topic of alcoholism and substance abuse is complex, and questions about susceptibility to addiction, addiction development, best methods of treatment, and the permanence of remission are still debated among experts.

The objective of this chapter to increase the understanding of problems faced by older homeless adult abusers. First, components of dependency are given, and the relationships between abuse and homelessness are discussed. Second, the incidence of alcohol and illegal drug abuse, as well as comorbidity, are clarified. Third, treatment modalities of the past and present are reviewed along with barriers to access. Physical and social problems associated with substance abuse and interventions for handling day-to-day encounters with homeless abusers are outlined.

COMPONENTS OF DEPENDENCY

Hauss (1988) defines the components of dependency as biochemical-genetic, psychological, and sociocultural, where usage is directly influenced by one's social circle. It is hotly debated whether alcoholism is a disease, whether one has control over it, and whether it is a behavioral disorder. Some people seem to have mastered the disease and to have quit drinking successfully. But the symptoms associated with withdrawal make one believe that there may be an organic cause (Wright, 1989).

Hauss (1988) points out attractive aspects of chemical dependency for a homeless person. These substances "can pick you up or slow you down; you can control mood changes" (p. 46), a state that may be a relief for the discomfort and distress associated with homelessness. Kelly and Cousineau (1990) add that this state becomes a coping mechanism that brings the homeless person close to euphoria. It becomes a way to get through the day or to forget failure (Institute of Medicine, 1988). It may also be used to keep the "unfriendly world at arms' length" (Wright, 1989, p. 103).

In older adults, two types of alcoholism exist: early and late-life onset. Because of medical and technological advances, many alcoholics now reach old age. Late-life onset can be triggered by losses, grief, loneliness, boredom, or pain (Butler, Lewis, & Sunderland, 1991). The older homeless adult may have been an alcohol abuser for a long time or may be a new abuser who is facing several losses. Atchley (1991) writes that "people who use too much alcohol are attempting to find a chemical solution to a human problem" (p. 268).

ALCOHOLISM AND HOMELESSNESS

The relationships between alcoholism and homelessness are complex. At one time migratory patterns and unemployment were thought to be the causes of alcoholism in the homeless. On the other hand, street life and skid row culture encouraged the consumption of alcohol (Stark, 1987). In a 1990 study, 6.7 percent of 181 homeless adults stated that alcoholism was the cause of their homelessness, 20 percent identified the cause with drug abuse, and 4.9 percent chose as a reason the combined use of alcohol and drugs, or alcohol or drug abuse associated with another reason (Spinner & Leaf, 1992). Among the 103 older homeless adults interviewed in the Tampa Bay area, almost 38 percent indicated that alcoholism was the cause of their homelessness (see the Appendix). As can be seen, chronic substance abuse may lead to homelessness, but homelessness may also lead to chronic abuse. Wright (1989) said that approximately one quarter of the homeless did not drink before they became homeless. Regardless of how alcoholism occurred, it can keep a person in the homeless situation (Bowdler, 1989).

PERSPECTIVES ON INCIDENCE

Homeless people have long been associated with severe and intractable alcohol disorders. Alcoholism is increasingly being recognized as their most pervasive health problem (Fisher & Breakey, 1991). Most homeless studies combine all types of abuse, making it difficult to determine the exact incidence of alcohol abuse versus prescribed and illicit drug abuse.

Several issues are raised when one evaluates the incidence of alcohol abuse among the homeless. Most studies of alcohol abuse are based on very different populations. Additionally, studies are done by different disciplines, each using different measures of alcohol abuse (Wright, 1989). Table 6.1 shows the differences in the percentage of males in the samples of each study, a factor that may greatly influence the results. Generally it is shown that the fewer males, the lower the incidence because of the low alcohol usage among women. Table 6.1 also reveals the narrowness of each sample; for example, the population may include only homeless in shelters or veterans. Reported rates of abuse, therefore, vary considerably and cannot be generalized to the entire population of homeless persons.

The stereotype of the homeless person as a single, middle-aged male alcoholic still persists. This stereotype links alcohol abuse and homelessness in the mind of the general population and leads to the popular description of the alcohol-impaired skid row bum. Currently, alcohol abuse is only one among many contributing factors of homelessness (Wright, 1989). The old stereotype does not reflect the new heterogeneous homeless population (Institute of Medicine, 1988), which now includes a higher proportion of women and minorities, families and children, older adults, and those with mental illness. Earlier findings on alcohol problems may not reflect this demographic change (Institute of Medicine, 1988). "In most cases, the homeless alcohol-dependent persons of today do not conform to the old skid-row stereotype, although those older, heavily dependent men still constitute one subgroup" (Fisher & Breakey, 1991, p. 1119).

Beginning in the 1900s, studies indicated a 30 to 33 percent incidence of alcohol-related problems among the homeless. This rate remained constant until 1986. At that time, the incidence increased and became much higher than in the general population. Although it involved a minority of the total population of the homeless, the "homeless remained associated with drinking, providing the impression that all homeless men were alcoholics and derelicts" (Kelly & Cousineau, 1990, p. 205). A 1987 study in Los Angeles

Table 6.1
Reported Incidence of Alcohol Abuse In Different Homeless Surveys

	Sample size	% of men in sample	Incidence (%)	Survey site
Bowdler 1989	90	42.0	17.0	Richmond, VA
Dowell & Farmer 1992	178	87.0	48.0	Long Beach, CA
Fisher & Breakey* 1990	295 232	100.0 0.0	66.8 28.3	MD shelter and jail
Koegel et al. 1988	328	95.4	62.9	LA shelters and services
Rich et al.** 1994	103	85.0	54.4	Tampa Bay
Regier et al 1988	18,571	41.0	13.3	5 cities
Rosenheck et al.* 1988	1188	98.0	58.3	Veterans Admin.
Spinner & Leaf 1992	181	91.7	53.3	New Haven, CT
Susser et al. 1989	678	100.0	36.0	NY shelters
Vernez et al.* 1988	315	62.0	57.0	CA shelters and streets

*In Fisher and Breakey (1991).
**See the Appendix.

showed that older unattached white males with an unsuccessful marriage history were the major segment of the alcohol-only group (Kelly & Cousineau, 1990). The rate of alcohol problems among the homeless is now estimated at between 25 and 40 percent, a rate much higher than that of the general population (Institute of Medicine, 1988). It is assumed that alcohol abuse is three to four times more prevalent in the homeless than in the housed population (Institute of Medicine, 1988; Wright, 1989).

A few studies report a 3 to 1 differential in homeless men and women problem drinkers. The pattern of drinking is curvilinear, with peak drinking appearing in middle age (30 to 64). The highest rate of alcohol abuse (60 percent or more) is found among homeless American Indians; the rate of drinking among homeless Hispanics and Asians is below average; and there are no substantial differences between the rate of abuse of whites and blacks (Wright, 1989).

Most homeless studies combine alcohol and drug abuse under the title of substance abuse; less attention has been given to drug abuse among the homeless than to alcohol abuse. The habit is costly, and the homeless person may not be able to maintain it. The rate of drug abuse may be ten to sixteen percent. Intravenous abuse, which is more likely to expose abusers to HIV/AIDS, is estimated at seven to eight percent among the homeless population. In order of prevalence, abuse is most frequent among black males, Hispanic males, black females, and white males. Since the rate of alcohol and drug abuse is lower among adult members of homeless families than among homeless living alone, this makes young black men the group at highest risk (Wright, 1989).

The Institute of Medicine (1988) reports that drug abuse drops after age 50; at the time of that survey, drug abuse was primarily seen on the East Coast. Spinner and Leaf (1992) found a high usage rate among a group of 181 homeless living in five emergency shelters in New Haven, Connecticut. This population showed 57 percent use among men and 27 percent use among women in the previous 30 days; 63.4 percent of them had used drugs during the previous year. Those who had been homeless for less than six months or more than four years were not using drugs as much as the others. Spinner and Leaf cite several hypotheses for the higher percentage of use among their sample: demographics (there are more young men and women drug abusers who have become homeless and are seeking shelters); increased prevalence of drug use in the nation; an increased preference among homeless persons to use drugs other than alcohol; and, finally the higher percentage of drug use may be unique to New Haven. Spinner and Leaf (1992) caution not to generalize the results to women since their representation in the sample was very small (15 women), and they also caution not to generalize to the homeless population because of the nature of the subgroup studied. They state that "the prevalence of substance abuse among homeless persons living in the street may, in fact, be higher than among the study sample" (p. 168). A comparison of the most recent rates is shown in Table 6.2. One must be cautious in evaluating these statistics because of the diversity in samples and sampling methods.

Wright, Knight, Weber-Burding, and Lam (1987) report on the drugs of choice among the 16 percent of users with a moderate to disabling drug problem in a group of 979 Ohio homeless adults. Heroine, methadone, or crack was the first choice for 37 percent of the abusers, cocaine for 22 percent, and marijuana for another 21 percent. Twenty percent used other street drugs such as amphetamines, depressants, PCP, etc. In two studies--one of homeless living on the street and one of those living in shelters--the drugs of choice were, respectively, marijuana followed by all forms of cocaine, and cocaine followed by marijuana. Only a small percentage in both studies used other street drugs (Dowell & Farmer, 1992; Spinner & Leaf, 1992). One may conclude that availability, cost, and ease of use are important factors in the drug of choice but that all forms of cocaine and marijuana are in greatest demand.

The Institute of Medicine (1988) quoted a study by Rosenheck et al., that used a sample drawn from the Veterans Administration Homeless Chronically Mentally Ill Program: Thirty-two percent of the homeless studied had alcohol and drug abuse problems; and 64 percent had been hospitalized for mental illness, alcoholism, or drug abuse. Because the total number of hospitalizations was less than the sum of the hospitalization for each diagnosis, one can believe that many hospitalizations were for dual or multiple diagnosis.

Wright (1989) estimates that "between one half to two thirds of the homeless have one or more of these three problems, and that perhaps one quarter have two or more of them" (pp. 108-109). He adds that the combination of mental illness and alcoholism seems to be more common. The highest rate of co-occurrence is found among blacks, then among American Indians, and finally among whites. The lowest rate is among Hispanics and Asians. "The presence of any one of these three disorders increases the likelihood that the remaining two will also be present" (p. 109).

Drake, Osher, and Wallach (1991) provide an overview of 10 studies that differentiate between homeless individuals with a single diagnosis and those with a dual diagnosis. The following ranges are reported: alcohol and mental disorder--3.6 to 26 percent; other drugs and mental disorders--1.7 to 2.5 percent; alcohol, drug, and mental disorder--8.0 to 31.1 percent. These dually diagnosed persons were primarily found to be in the older homeless males, were less likely to be working, had a long history of homelessness, and lived primarily on the streets.

Recent studies of alcohol and drug patterns among older homeless adults are difficult to find. A few studies report alcohol problems ranging from 30.1 to 37.5 percent among those 50 to 64 years age group and from 1.1 to 18.1 percent in the age group 65+. Studies of comorbidity do not separate

Table 6.2
Reported Incidence of Drug Abuse In Different Homeless Surveys

	Sample size	% of men in sample	Incidence (%)	Survey site
Bowdler 1989	90	42.0	3.0	Richmond, VA
Breakey et al. 1989	203	62.5	20.1	Baltimore shelters
Dowell & Farmer 1992	178	87.0	40.0	Long Beach, CA
Koegel et al. 1988	328	95.4	30.8	LA shelters and services
Rich et al.* 1994	103	85.0	7.8	Tampa Bay
Regier et al 1988	18,571	41.0	5.9	5 cities
Spinner & Leaf 1992	181	91.7	54.0	New Haven, CT
Susser et al. 1989	221	100.0	38.0	NY shelters
Toro & Wall** 1989	76	79.0	37.1	Buffalo shelters and streets

*See the Appendix.
**In Fisher and Breakey (1991).

older homeless adults from the homeless adult group. The Tampa Bay survey reveals alcohol usage in 54.4 percent of the 103 older homeless adults 50+. This is in the higher range of use by the adult homeless population.

There are several reasons that the results of the Tampa Bay survey cannot be generalized. First, over 50 percent of the participants were veterans; as shown in a study by Koegel, Burnam and Farr (1988), homeless veterans have a higher alcohol abuse/dependence (73.2 percent) than nonhomeless veterans (57.8 percent). This would lead us to conclude that the results of the Tampa Bay survey may overestimate the actual alcohol use rate among older homeless adults. A second factor preventing generalization is a sample that was not random, and a third is a sample size in the 65+ group that was very small (12). However, we may still compare these results with those existing in the literature if we do not generalize. Of interest is the fact that among the seven clients who reported using illegal drugs, only one did not have a triple diagnosis of alcohol abuse, drug abuse, and mental illness.

Butler et al. (1991) report that the incidence of alcoholism among older adults is higher among males, especially widowers. There is a high frequency of drinking among veterans who were exposed to war experiences and the cultural drinking pattern of the armed forces. Butler et al. add that alcoholism is difficult to diagnose in older adults for two reasons: (1) They do not have the opportunity to drink socially as other groups do; and (2) the symptoms of alcoholism may be easily overlooked and/or attributed to physiological changes of aging. Atchley (1991) writes that among a group of older alcoholics admitted for treatment in a Texas psychiatric screening agency, 60 percent were suffering from some degree of organic brain disease.

Most older adults using illegal drugs began in early adulthood. It is difficult to detect drug use in older adults because they are more adept at avoiding detection. It is expected that in the near future the rate of abuse may increase because a large proportion of drug abusers were young adults in the 1960s when illegal drug use increased dramatically (Atchley, 1991).

PERSPECTIVES ON TREATMENT MODALITIES

Historically, the treatment of a homeless alcoholic was incarceration. McCarthy, Argeriou, Huebner, and Lubran (1991) write that "services for homeless inebriates changed little from 1800 through 1940. Almshouses, shelters, and jails were the primary institutions for the indigent and derelict" (p. 1141). After 1951, when the American Medical Association defined alcoholism as a disease, there was more emphasis on treatment methods. The 1971 Uniform Alcoholism and Intoxication Treatment Act established standards for treatment and rehabilitation programs. At that time, hospital-based programs began to serve alcohol dependents. Thomas, Kelly, and Cousineau (1990) state that because medical models are always expensive and rarely serve the indigent, a less expensive social model began to emerge. Dowell and Farmer (1992) explain that as a response to the McKinney Act, a national demonstration program called National Institute on Alcohol Abuse and Alcoholism and the National Institute on Drug Abuse (NIAAA/NIDA) was initiated in 1988. Its objective was to evaluate a variety of community-based service models for treatment of homeless with an alcohol or drug problem. The federal government's war on drugs seems to bring us back to the first treatment modality, treatment by time in jail (Thomas et al., 1990).

ALTERNATIVE TREATMENTS

There are several demonstration projects currently being tested: sobering-up stations, outreach, case management, treatment linked with housing, restriction on availability of abusing substances; and alcohol- and drug-free housing--the Oxford House model; the Cleveland, Ohio model; and the recovery model (McCarthy et al., 1991; Kelly & Cousineau, 1990; National Institute on Alcohol Abuse and Alcoholism, 1991).

Sobering-up stations accept intoxicated persons at any time, day or night. "They are alternatives to life on the streets or time in the county jail" (McCarthy et al., 1991, p. 1143). They serve as the first point of contact for the homeless with an alcohol or drug problem.

The *outreach method* sends paraprofessionals and professionals to the environment of the homeless person. They make contact with the alcohol or drug abuser and offer food, shelter, and information on alcohol and drug treatment opportunities. This alternative improves access to care.

Case management provides for coordination of care and development of interorganizational links. In the treatment of alcohol and drug abuse, the case manager evaluates individual needs, facilitates access to community resources, and encourages individual development of problem-solving skills and appropriate coping mechanisms. Such projects also utilize multiagency groups, public forums, and formal interorganizational agreements to strengthen the service supports.

Treatment linked with housing is an important part of the treatment system. One center offers a three-month treatment program in a rural facility followed by a four-month stay in an urban transitional center. In this later stage, the recovering homeless person is encouraged to find permanent housing, to develop work-related skills, and to establish a supportive network to maintain alcohol-free living. Another center is especially designed for homeless mothers and offers on-site living for children. In addition to substance abuse treatment, the mothers receive training in parenting skills, money management, and job training. Other programs add nutrition education, housekeeping, and hygiene education. A $2 million federal grant will help launch a new residential program in Tampa, Florida. This transitional 50-bed home will accept homeless persons with mental health and substance abuse problems. Clients will receive counseling, basic medical care, and job training. The goal is to have clients progress from having no support to developing all the internal strengths they can (Drayton, 1991).

Restricting access to alcohol or other drugs has been tried in skid row areas (one in Portland, Oregon and one in San Francisco, California). These programs appeared to have reduced intoxication and the problems associated with skid row life. They were, however, insufficient to address the problems of alcohol and drug abuse.

Alcohol and drug-free housing is provided by Oxford House, Inc. in Silver Springs, Maryland. This is a multisite nonprofit corporation that offers group housing for alcoholics and drug addicts and is an inexpensive method of partially fulfilling the need for sober housing. The houses, financed with rental payments, are located in neighborhood environments. Most of the group living arrangements are for men only. There are no managers or counselors. Strict rules and regulations are monitored by residents, whose major responsibility is to enforce sobriety. Failure to adhere results in immediate expulsion; occupants are given instructions on the management of finances and are accountable for themselves. There are two conditions for entrance: (1) Members must have income, although welfare clients are accepted as long as they actively look for permanent employment; and (2) applicants must have a 30-day history of sobriety. Lodges, single-room occupancy hotels, and congregate facilities with on-site services are the second best alternatives.

The Cleveland, Ohio Model uses a substance abuse counselor with the existing medical team working in emergency shelters, soup kitchens, and other sites. A contract with existing facilities in the community provides two different programs at a fixed fee per service: one program for alcoholics and another for drug abusers. The Cleveland model is based on the Twelve Steps of Alcoholics Anonymous. A case manager is assigned to the client to handle such problems as clothing, acquisition of personal items, transportation, acceptance in a general assistance program, and housing and furnishings for the posttreatment period.

The recovery model program works for many. This program is a therapeutic peergroup experience, following the "helper-therapy" where the helper receives as much help as the person being helped (Kelly & Cousineau, 1990). This program is known as Alcoholics, Cocaine, or Narcotics Anonymous. The clients are as involved in recovery as they were in addiction. The program offers life coping strategies to replace alcohol.

BARRIERS TO TREATMENT AND CONTINUED SOBRIETY

There are several barriers to the treatment of substance abuse and the maintenance of sobriety. Among them are client denial, environment, the nature of the problem, the availability of treatment beds, social response to homeless abusers, special problems of comorbidity, the added problems of older homeless adults, the lack of positive reinforcement after detoxification, and finally, but not least, cost. A brief overview of barriers follows.

The client uses denial to refuse to acknowledge that a problem exists. This leads to an unconscious construction of excuses or rationalization followed by belief in the fabricated stories. Homeless adults may have a great interest in protecting a defense mechanism that renders life more bearable (Hauss, 1988). Many who experience homelessness for a few months might conclude that alcoholism is a useful, convenient, and relatively cheap coping mechanism. The temporary illusion of well-being is "an improvement over the long-term reality of daily existence for many of these people" (Wright, 1989, p. 100).

The homeless person deciding to enter a treatment program does not know where to live before, during, or after treatment. Being sober and homeless is a poor combination because the drinking/drug-abusing environment negates the positive aspects of treatment. The homeless in recovery must cope with problems of housing, employment, and entitlement. This lack of resources has been identified as the most critical problem and is often a devastating one for the recovering homeless (Kelly & Cousineau, 1990).

Kelly and Cousineau (1990) write that "recovery is a journey, and after a while it becomes a way of life. The descent into addiction, homelessness, and poor health often takes years to achieve. The recovery process takes years to practice" (p. 211). The most difficult task is convincing clients that they cannot recover unless they avoid these chemicals *forever*. Because relapses occur in one half to two thirds, addicts suffer greatly. When the alcoholic returns to the street, which is typical, the programs can have but limited success. Many trials will, therefore, be made at enormous expense to society (Wright, 1989).

Public beds are always full, and there is little funding for additional treatment beds or halfway houses. There are long delays before a person can be placed in a detoxification or rehabilitation program. Consequently, motivation to attend the program has often waned and it may be impossible to persuade the client to take advantage of the presenting opportunity (Wright, 1989).

The incidence of alcoholism, drug abuse, and mental illness in the homeless population may encourage a negative use of the data by nonsympathetic persons. It may also be used to blame the homeless abusers for their fate and increase prejudice. This further lowers public support for services (Fisher & Breakey, 1991). Some projects funded by NIAAA/NIDA have faced considerable community resistance because of the population being served and the nature of the proposed interventions. Sobering-up stations and women's residential programs were the most opposed (McCarthy et al., 1991).

Dually diagnosed clients are the most difficult to engage in treatment and the most difficult to treat. Therefore, caregivers are reluctant to embrace the challenge (McCarthy et al., 1991). Many mental health facilities refuse treatment to alcoholics and many alcohol and drug rehabilitation facilities refuse treatment to mentally ill individuals. Few facilities have clinicians trained in both mental health and substance abuse treatment (Drake et al., 1991). The reluctance to accept these clients comes from their unpredictable, problematic behavior, medical problems and high risks, and their demanding attitude (McCarthy et al., 1991). These individuals are at increased risk of not being treated and, therefore, will become worse and less tolerated (Burt, 1992).

Older homeless adults have additional problems. Atchley (1991) writes that alcoholic older homeless adults tend to be ignored by law enforcement unless they create a disturbance. They are, therefore, less likely to be treated except when severely ill. Ageism leads also to fewer treatment referrals. It is difficult to diagnose alcoholism among older adults because they drink more privately than socially, and their symptoms are often attributed to physiological changes of age or senile dementia. Illegal drug use is also more difficult to diagnose. Older adults do not generally volunteer information, and years of usage have made them more adept at avoiding detection.

Few programs offer the social support and reinforcement necessary to maintain sobriety. Cleveland offers a special job-training and job-seeking skills program for homeless persons who remain sober for 90 days after completing a chemical dependency program. A two-week job evaluation workshop; a training program followed by adult education, if needed, or direct assignment to a full-time job with full medical benefits is part of the program. A counselor helps with clothes and lunches and encourages clients after a bad day (Kelly & Cousineau, 1990). Some areas have shelters specifically designed for homeless people who are alcoholics or drug abusers.

States and communities in poor economic times are reluctant to support development of multifaceted comprehensive programs such as those needed for the treatment of alcohol and drug abuse in the homeless population (McCarthy et al., 1991). Society may not consider the rate of treatment success to be worth the cost.

PHYSICAL AND SOCIAL PROBLEMS

Substance abuse greatly adds to the physical, social, and mental health problems of the homeless (Hauss, 1988). Alcohol abusers are more prone to serious physical illnesses. Common diseases include nutritional deficiencies, injuries, serious upper respiratory infections, liver disease, seizure disorders, diabetes, anemia, neurological disorders, eye disorders and diseases, cardiac disease and hypertension, chronic obstructive pulmonary disease, arthritis, and active tuberculosis. Alcohol abuse is also indicative of premature mortality in many homeless people (Wright, 1989).

Substance abusers are prone to HIV/AIDS. There is no clear comparison between the incidence of this disease among the homeless and the remainder of the drug-abusing population. As the incidence increases in the general population, it is expected that it will increase among the homeless. Older adults are also among those infected with HIV/AIDS. Other prevalent diseases are hepatitis, abscesses, thrombophlebitis, and bacterial endocarditis (Institute of Medicine, 1988). Wright (1989) adds that all categories of sexually transmitted diseases are more prevalent in this group. Since many of these people also abuse alcohol, they experience many of the alcohol-related diseases as well.

Another problem is thermoregulation, regulation of body temperature. Alcohol causes vasodilation of small peripheral vessels and may directly affect the cerebral heat regulation center. Older homeless adults, who often have peripheral circulatory problems, are at increased risk. In the winter, vasodilation accentuates heat loss and may lead to a higher incidence of hypothermia (Milhorn & Gardner, 1990) and frostbite. During the summer, vasodilation increases absorption of heat from the environment, and more frequent heat strokes may be experienced.

Older adults, 55+, are more severely affected by alcohol. There are several changes in the physiological tolerance to alcohol, and recovery is significantly slower. Older adults have a smaller proportion of body water. Therefore, a small amount of alcohol results in a higher blood level (Milhorn & Gardner, 1990), and death is possible with a surprisingly low level of alcohol. Elimination is much slower; younger adults may process one ounce of alcohol in one hour, but older adults may take three to four times longer to process the same quantity. Butler et al. (1991) write that the confusion, forgetfulness, and belligerent behavior associated with alcoholism may mimic severe somatic mental health syndromes. They add that chronic alcoholism greatly impairs behavior and memory and increases the risk of delirium tremens, alcohol dementia, and Korsakoff psychosis. Twenty-five to sixty percent of dementia is caused by alcoholism, and depression in older adults is often the result of alcohol use (Milhorn & Gardner, 1990). Cardiac function is impaired, angina is more difficult to discern, pulmonary function is lowered, nutritional deficiencies are frequent, dehydration becomes a problem for frail older adults, and combination of alcohol and drugs can result in respiratory depression and death (Milhorn & Gardner, 1990).

Abusers are "more socially disaffiliated, more profoundly disabled, more impoverished, and much sicker; . . . they are rated . . . as having by far the worst chances for the future, as being the least employable, and as most likely to be chronically homeless" (Wright, 1989, p. 99). It is difficult for them to obtain sympathy because they are believed responsible for their fate. As the level of disability mounts, housing and job possibilities diminish. They are considered undesirable patients by many health-care and social-service institutions. With multiple diagnosis they are considered even more undesirable, and the mentally ill are the most undesirable of all. "To be drunk, crazy, and homeless is about as low as one can fall" (Wright, 1989, p. 110).

DAY-TO-DAY ENCOUNTERS WITH OLDER HOMELESS ADULTS

Service providers are the initial contact persons for older homeless adults with a problem of substance abuse. They can help identify the abusers, learn to recognize withdrawal symptoms, bring awareness about the relationship of illness and substance abuse, work with the social consequences of abuse, and handle crisis interventions. Some suggested interventions compiled from articles of Hauss (1988) and Houston (1989) follow.

1. Develop and be consistent with shelter rules.
2. Learn sources of assistance, such as AA (Alcoholics Anonymous), GA (Gamblers Anonymous), Al-Anon (for relatives and spouses of alcoholics), NA (Narcotics Anonymous), and DA (Drugs Anonymous). A mailing list of resources on the topic of the homeless with alcohol problems and a report on "sober hotels" or alcohol-free living centers is also available from the National Institute on Alcoholism, 5600 Fishers Lane, Rockdale, MD 20857.
3. Offer support in decisions to get help by communicating the continuing option for substance abuse treatment.
4. Communicate a sense of acceptance and encourage responsibility for self-health.
5. Avoid confrontation or accusations.
6. Be realistic. Base on individual functional level.
7. Keep in touch with the person during the treatment.
8. Help the client develop alternative coping mechanisms. Reestablishing social support or finding substitute support

is important to decrease isolation and alienation from society.

9. Do not fall into an "enabler's role" by feeling pity for the substance abuser or covering up negative behaviors.
10. Place responsibility in the hands of the abuser. You can only provide help and support.

When the client is in a state of inebriation or withdrawal,

1. Be aware of your own reactions, or you may become angry and defensive, thus exacerbating the client's mood swings.
2. Obtain support from another staff person if the client becomes aggressive.
3. If the client is disoriented or hallucinating, keep the area well lit with doors closed. Shut out loud noises and interruptions.
4. Do not argue with the client. Allow the person to speak freely. Only one staff member should speak.
5. Be prepared to use medical backup when the client is in withdrawal, which is a medical emergency.

Among older adults, symptoms of alcoholism are insomnia; impotence; problems with control of gout; rapid onset of confusional state; uncontrollable hypertension; unexplained falls/bruises; excessive sleepiness; flushed face; bloated appearance; anemia; and depression (Butler et al., 1991). Other clues are neglect of appearance and hygiene; cigarette burns; attempts to talk about suicide; frequent behavior/mood changes; and frequent health complaints. Remember that each time a client experiences withdrawal, the symptoms are likely to be worse than the time before.

SUMMARY

Substance abuse in older homeless adults is a complex problem. Research is needed to clarify causes and incidence and to develop appropriate treatment. Service providers must be astute to recognize substance abuse. They should avoid labeling the older adult's behavior as "normal for their age," because memory loss, unsteady gait, confusion, disorientation, falls, and hostility may be clues to alcoholism as well as other problems. It is also important to remember that many older homeless adults may have a life-long alcohol habit and that older persons can be adept at hiding their habits. Older adults may be seen by helping professionals only when they do not exhibit symptoms or when they are critically ill. In the near future, it is likely that drug abuse among older adults will be on the increase because of earlier habits. Detection will become a task of greater importance.

The literature suggests that older homeless adults are at greater risk for comorbidity, and that age-related changes increase the likelihood of detrimental physical and mental affects of abusive substances. In addition, older adults cannot get around easily and are more prone to victimization. These additional risk factors place them at a greater disadvantage than younger homeless. Furthermore, older adults are more likely to be ignored by law enforcement, to be unsupported by public entitlement, and to sleep on the street.

REFERENCES

Atchley, R. C. (1991). *Social forces and aging*. Belmont, CA: Wadsworth Publishing Company.

Bowdler, J. R. (1989). Health problems of the homeless in America. *Nurse Practitioner*, *14*(7), 44-51.

Breakey, W. R., Fisher, P. J., Kramer, M., Nestadt, G., Romanoski, A. J., Ross, A., Royall, R. M., & Stene, O. (1989). Health and mental problems of homeless men and women in Baltimore. *Journal of the American Medical Association*, *262*, 1352-1357.

Burt, M. R. (1992). *Over the edge: The growth of homelessness in the 1980s*. New York: Russell Sage Foundation.

Butler, R. N., Lewis, M. I., & Sunderland, T. (1991). *Aging and mental health*. New York: MacMillan.

Dowell, D. A., & Farmer, F. (1992). Community response to homelessness: Social change and constraint in local intervention. *Journal of Community Psychology*, *20*, 72-83.

Drake, R. E., Osher, F. C., & Wallach, M. A. (1991). Homelessness and dual diagnosis. *American Psychologist*, *46*(11), 1149-1158.

Drayton, M. (1991, October 27). Grant may boost new facility for homeless. *The Tampa Tribune*, *North Tampa Section*, p. 1.

Fisher, P. J. & Breakey, W. R. (1991). The epidemiology of alcohol, drug, and mental disorders among homeless persons. *American Psychologist*, *46*(11), 1115-1128.

Hauss, A. (Ed). (1988). *Working with homeless people*. New York: Columbia University Community Services.

Houston, M. K. (1989). Substance abuse. In T. L. Boaz & M. Kunkel (Eds.), *Working with the homeless mentally ill: A resource manual for caregivers* (pp. 83-108). Tampa, FL: University of South Florida, Florida Mental Health Institute.

Institute of Medicine. Committee on Health Care for Homeless People. (1988). *Homelessness, health, and human needs.* Washington, DC: National Academy Press.

Kelly, T. L., & Cousineau, M. (1990). Alcoholism and substance abuse. In P. W. Brickner, L. K. Scharer, B. Conanan, M. Savarese, & B. C. Scanlan (Eds.), *Under the safety net: The health and social welfare of the homeless in the United States* (pp. 204-214). New York: W. W. Norton.

Koegel, P. J., Burnam, M. A., & Farr, R. K. (1988). The prevalence of specific psychiatric disorders among homeless individuals in the inner-city of Los Angeles. *Archives of General Psychiatry, 45*, 1085-1092.

McCarthy, D., Argeriou, M., Huebner, R. B., & Lubran, B. (1991). Alcoholism, drug abuse, and the homeless. *American Psychologist, 46*(11), 1139-1149.

Milhorn, M. T., & Gardner, L. C. (1990, July). When to suspect alcoholism: How to help when you do. *Senior Patient,* pp. 41-44.

National Institute on Alcohol Abuse and Alcoholism. (1991). *Synopses of cooperative agreements for research demonstration projects on alcohol and other drug abuse treatment for homeless persons* (DHHS Publication No. ADM 91-1763). Washington, DC: U.S. Government Printing Office.

Regier, D. A., Boyd, J. H., & Burke, J. D. (1988). One-month prevalence of mental disorders in the United States: Based on five epidemiologic catchment area sites. *Archives of General Psychiatry, 45*, 977-986.

Spinner, G. F., & Leaf, P. J. (1992). Homelessness and drug abuse in New Haven. *Hospital and Community Psychiatry, 43*(2), 166-168.

Stark, L. (1987). A century of alcohol and homelessness. *Alcohol Health & Research World, 11*(3), 8-13.

Susser, E., Struening, E. L., & Conover, S. (1989). Psychiatric problems in homeless men. *Archives of General Hospital and Community Psychiatry, 40*, 261-265.

Thomas, L., Kelly, M., & Cousineau, M. (1990). Alcoholism and substance abuse. In P. W. Brickner, L. K. Scharer, B. Conanan, M. Savarese, & B. C. Scanlan (Eds.), *Under the safety net: The health and social welfare of the homeless in the United States* (pp. 204-214). New York: W. W. Norton.

Williams, G. D., Stenson, F. S., Parker, D. A., Harford, T. C., & Noble, J. (1987). Demographic trends, alcohol abuse and alcoholism. *Alcohol Health & Research World, 11*(3), 80-83.

Wright, J. D. (1989). *Address unknown.* New York: Aldine de Gruyter.

Wright, J. D., Knight, J. W., Weber-Burding, E., & Lam, J. (1987). Ailments and alcohol: Health status among the drinking homeless. *Alcohol Health & Research World, 11*(3), 22-27.

7

Physical Health Issues

Irena M. Zuk

Although it is comparable to the health problems of older adults in general, the health of older homeless adults is aggravated by severe living conditions, poor nutrition, lack of proper sleeping arrangements, lack of health care, and extreme stress from living on the streets.

BACKGROUND

According to Robertson and Cousineau (1986), 34 percent of the homeless surveyed rated their health as fair to poor, 38 percent of these reported having at least one chronic health problem (63 percent of women reporting in contrast to 32 percent of the men). Tessler and Dennis (1989) show a wide range of statistics, with 12 to 50 percent indicating poor health. These authors believe, however, that one third to one half is the accurate estimate.

Although only 12 percent of the homeless surveyed in Detroit reported poor health (Tessler & Dennis, 1989), it was found that 72 percent needed glasses, 63 percent required dental work, and 40 to 50 percent had one or more cardiovascular, gastrointestinal, respiratory, or musculoskeletal problem.

Homelessness brings with it an overall deterioration of physical health, especially for the older adult, for whom health care is one of the most urgent problems. Being on the street all day or walking to the nearest place to get a meal can be especially hard on the older adult who may be suffering from arthritis or ulcerations of the feet and legs. Brickner, Scanlan, Conanan, Elvy, McAdam, Scharer, and Vicic (1986) and Doolin (1985) report that it is difficult to keep clean and that the homeless are at considerable risk for lice, scabies, and infectious diseases, including tuberculosis. Older adults are particularly prone to thermoregulatory problems, and if they are on psychotropic medications, these can lead to further thermoregulatory disorders (Goldfrank, 1985). Respiratory illnesses such as colds, sore throat, bronchitis, and flu are common.

MAJOR MEDICAL PROBLEMS

Older homeless adults have major medical problems, such as hypertension, tuberculosis, cardiac disease, osteoporosis, musculoskeletal infections, diabetes, arthritis, respiratory illnesses, malnutrition, HIV/AIDS, mental health problems, and alcohol and drug abuse as well as varying degrees of trauma.

Hypertension and *coronary artery disease* are related to poor diet and are therefore difficult to treat (Winick, 1985). Hypertension requires ongoing care, which is seldom available to the homeless (Kinchen & Wright, 1991). Lack of social supports which might encourage proper health care is a contributing factor and left untreated, hypertension can lead to stroke, heart disease, and kidney failure.

The incidence of *tuberculosis* is steadily increasing among the homeless, who may be noncompliant with treatment and who often find themselves in the close quarters of a shelter. The older homeless adult, subject to the stress of inadequate housing and nutrition, is at especially high risk (Brickner et al., 1986). Those 65+ have the highest prevalence rates (31 percent) of tuberculosis (for age 55 to 64 the rate is 20 percent; age 45 to 54, 18 percent; age 35 to 44, 14 percent; age 20 to 34, nine percent). Overall, the rate is 12.3 percent (Brickner et al., 1986).

Osteoporosis, the twelfth leading cause of death in the overall population, is extremely dangerous for older homeless adults, especially women (Winick, 1985). Although calcium intake cannot reverse this condition, it can slow deterioration. Vitamins are overlooked as a priority item and should be made available because nutritional needs are not being met.

Musculoskeletal infections, found mainly in the feet (Brickner et al., 1986; Noble, Scott, Cavicci, & Robinson, 1985), are exacerbated by frostbite, infection, and poorly fitting shoes. McBride and Mulcare (1985) describe chronic venous insufficiency, a stasis ulcer formation from which older homeless adults often suffer. The valves bridging the deep and superficial venous system are damaged or destroyed. Subsequently, red blood cells leak into surrounding tissue, inhibiting assimilation of oxygen and nutrients and hindering removal of waste. As the tissue is damaged and cells begin to die, a calf or thigh may swell to such a degree that it may prevent walking.

Diabetic foot ulcers are also very dangerous among older homeless adults (McBride & Mulcare, 1985). Because they are not able to store medication properly, homeless diabetics are much more susceptible to infection than those not exposed to life on the streets. Infection can spread rapidly from even small cuts, and without immediate treatment the outcome can be devastating, resulting in the loss of a limb or life.

Arthritis can be an extremely painful illness, producing joint stiffness, pain, discomfort, limited movement, and swelling. Emotions evoked are exhaustion, frustration, and depression (Khan & Fischer, 1991). These symptoms, along with homelessness and the necessity of being on the move, underscore the hardships of the older homeless person.

Respiratory illnesses, such as colds, sore throat, bronchitis, flu, and gastroenteritis, are common. Trauma from wounds which develop secondary infections is prevalent (Noble et al., 1985).

Malnutrition results from improper diet. Lack of food and shelter and loss of needed vitamins can cause deadly changes in the body (Winick, 1985). As fat tissue is depleted, muscle mass decreases, water loss occurs in cells, heart rate decreases, blood pressure drops, and body temperature falls below normal. The person suffering from this condition becomes apathetic, movements become slower, and activity decreases. As the efficiency of the immune system is undermined, the susceptibility to infection increases.

Causes of malnutrition in the older homeless adult, other than lack of funds, may be *dental problems*. Improper dentures or bad teeth can prevent proper chewing and lead to loss of taste and thereby little pleasure in eating (Khan & Fischer, 1991). Symptoms of malnutrition, overmedication, and depression are often misdiagnosed as dementia. Symptoms are similar: confusion about time and place, paranoia, withdrawal, outbursts of anger, and confusion in general. If treated in time, these symptoms can be reversed. Older adults who must take medications rarely have access to refrigeration for storage, if needed (Hudson, Rauch, Dawson, Santos, & Burdick, 1990), nor do they have the privilege of controlling their food intake according to sodium and caloric content. This exacerbates physical ailments.

The Center for the Study of Aging (1989) notes that skin sensitivity to temperature change increases with the aging process, and the older adult is beginning to, or already has, lost much insulating fat. In this regard the older homeless adult is at even higher risk.

MEDICAL TREATMENT

Although surveys show that 47 percent of older homeless adults could name a person or place to whom they would go for medical care, only 13 percent had a specific regular source of treatment. Of these, 35 percent named free clinics, 23 percent emergency rooms and 15 percent veterans' hospitals. Those who had no access to medical treatment said they had no need for it (24 percent) and lacked insurance (39 percent). Although 11 percent had suffered an injury or acute illness (29 percent) in the past two months, fewer than half (44 percent) had been in touch with a physician. Of those who had, 38 percent went to free clinics, 28 percent to emergency rooms, and 18 percent to community hospitals (Robertson & Cousineau, 1986). Twenty-three percent of those who did not seek help said they could not afford it, while 6 percent cited not having transportation. If they are able to travel, they risk getting back too late to sign into a shelter (Institute of Medicine, 1988).

Tessler and Dennis (1989) point out that because the homeless are without health insurance and preventive care, they wind up using the most expensive services--inpatient and emergency room services. Two thirds to four fifths were not covered by Medicaid, for which they might actually have been eligible. Unfortunately, because they do not have a regular residence, it is often difficult to obtain Medicaid or other government assistance.

INNOVATIONS

Reilly and McInnis (1985) describe the success of Pine Street Inn in Boston's South End. Pine Street Inn is an innovative emergency shelter with a clinic providing service evenings and weekends to 70 men and 25 women. Its special effort is to treat tuberculosis, with the goal of maintaining optimal health and follow-up. If clients do not show up for appointments, staff look for them. The treatment plan is written at the bottom of each referral sheet for other staff members and for agencies which may call seeking information on the patients. The clinic has a good relationship with local hospitals and agencies, and ongoing meetings take place with the different departments. Emergency room personnel, doctors, nurses, and social workers are invited to the shelter, and volunteers are recruited from among nursing and medical students. Some volunteers stay with one patient for a semester, adding a stable relationship to the lives of clients. Along with other researchers in this field, Brickner et al. (1986) call for an interdisciplinary team of doctors and counselors to treat older homeless adults.

REFERENCES

Brickner, P. W., Scanlan, B. C., Conanan, B., Elvy, A., McAdam, J., Scharer, L. K., & Vicic, W. J. (1986). Homeless persons and health care. *Annals of Internal Medicine 104*, 405-409.

Center for the Study of Aging. (1989). *Aging*. Tuscaloosa, AL: The University of Alabama, College of Community Health Sciences.

Doolin, J. (1985, March/April). "America's untouchables:" The elderly homeless. *Perspective on Aging*, pp. 8-11. Cited in *The new homeless crisis: Old and poor in the streets*. Hearing before the Select Committee on Aging, House of Representatives, Committee No.101-784, September 26, 1990 (pp. 96-99). Washington, DC.

Goldfrank, L. (1985). Exposure: Thermoregulatory disorders in the homeless patient. In P. W. Brickner, L. K. Scharer, B. Conanan, A. Elvy, & M. Savarese (Eds.), *Health care of homeless people* (pp. 57-76). New York: Springer-Verlag.

Hudson, B. A., Rauch, B. B., Dawson, G. D., Santos, J. F., & Burdick, D. C. (1990). *Homelessness: Special problems related to training, research, and the elderly*. Unpublished manuscript. University of Notre Dame, Department of Psychology, South Bend, IN.

Institute of Medicine, Committee on Health Care for Homeless People. (1988). *Homelessness, health, and human needs*. Washington, DC: National Academy Press.

Khan, L. N., & Fischer, H. (1991). *Frequent health problems of the elderly*. Philadelphia: Philadelphia Geriatric Center, Baer Consultation and Diagnostic Center.

Kinchen, K., & Wright, J. D. (1991). Hypertension management in health care for the homeless clinics: Results from a survey. *American Journal of Public Health*, *81*,(9), 1163-1165.

McBride, K., & Mulcare, R. J. (1985). Peripheral vascular disease in the homeless. In P. W. Brickner, L. K. Scharer, B. Conanan, A. Elvy, & M. Savarese (Eds.), *Health care of homeless people* (pp. 121-130). New York: Springer-Verlag.

Noble, J., Scott, T., Cavicci, L., & Robinson, P. E. (1985). The problem of infections: The experience of the city of Boston's shelter for the homeless. In P. W. Brickner, L. K. Scharer, B. Conanan, A. Elvy, & M. Savarese (Eds.), *Health care of homeless people* (pp. 93-102). New York: Springer-Verlag.

Reilly, E., & McInnis, B. (1985). Boston, Massachusetts: The Pine Street Inn Nurses' Clinic and Tuberculosis Program. In P. W. Brickner, L. K. Scharer, B. Conanan, A. Elvy, & M. Savarese (Eds.), *Health care of homeless people* (pp. 291-300). New York: Springer-Verlag.

Robertson, M. J., & Cousineau, M. R. (May). Health status and access to health services among the urban homeless. *American Journal of Public Health*, *76*(5), 561-563.

Tessler, R. C., & Dennis, D. L. (1989). *A Synthesis of NIMH-Funded Research concerning persons who are homeless and mentally ill*. Program for the Homeless Mentally Ill. Division of Education and Service Systems Liaison. Washington, DC: National Institute of Mental Health Press.

Winick, M. (1985). Nutritional and vitamin deficiency states. In P. W. Brickner, L. K. Scharer, B. Conanan, A. Elvy, & M. Savarese (Eds.), *Health care of homeless people* (pp. 103-108). New York: Springer-Verlag.

8

Medication: Overview and Issues

Louisette A. Boucher

Pharmacology, the scientific study of medicinal drugs and their effects on the body, is a complex subject. Each medication has its own array of possible side effects, precautions, and recommended dosages. Individual reactions to treatment regimens are not well understood, especially in women and older adults. Nevertheless, a general knowledge of medication patterns, compliance problems, drug side effects, interactions, and precautions is important for understanding and facilitating drug treatment. This knowledge is the basis for better assessment of client situations and appropriate decision making. Additionally, the information can be used for client education and, in the event of homelessness, for encouraging safe and effective methods of compliance with a medication regimen in a hazardous environment. Each of these topics will be discussed to assist in the evaluation of the differing needs and interventions required to help homeless adults, and particularly older homeless adults.

MEDICATION PATTERNS

Solomon, White, Parron, and Mendelson (1979) write that our society is an "overmedicated society," a view supported by substantial evidence. Medication patterns in the general population raise major concerns. These include drug use in the youth culture, barbiturate and tranquilizer use, and alcohol use and abuse in the middle-aged. The older adult population has its own medication problems. Although people 60+ make up 16.7 percent of the population, they consume almost 40 percent of prescribed medications in the United States (Wolfe & Hope, 1993). It is also evident that medication patterns vary among ages. Twenty-five percent of older adults have prescriptions for six or more drugs; only 3 percent of younger adults have as many. Furthermore, over-the-counter drugs are used by 70 percent of those 60+, compared to a 10 percent use by the general population (Butler, Lewis, & Sunderland, 1991).

Literature is sparse on the subject of medication use among the homeless. Bowdler (1989) reports on the medication usage of 77 homeless persons seen at the Cross-Over Health Clinic in Richmond, Virginia. Table 8.1 shows the medications dispensed by order of frequency for this group of homeless.

Table 8.1
Cross-Over Health Clinic, Richmond, Va.

Type	Percentage
Antibiotics	72%
Respiratory/antihistamine	33%
Anti-inflammatory/pain	32%
Miscellaneous	18%
Vitamins/metabolites	15%
Cardiac/antihypertensive	14%
Neuroleptics/tranquilizers	12%
Gastrointestinal	5%
Hypoglycemics	5%

The U. S. Department of Housing and Urban Development (1984) estimates that about 6 percent of homeless people nationwide are age 60+ (Kutza & Keigher, 1991). In Florida, the state with the highest percentage of older adults, a street-based survey identified 12 to 15 percent of the homeless to be over 55 (Hillsborough County, 1990). It is important to review the medication patterns of older adults and integrate this knowledge into that of the general homeless adult population.

Wolfe and Hope (1993) report that 61 percent of domiciled persons age 65+ (not in nursing homes or hospitals) receive three or more prescription drugs; 37 percent receive five or more; and 19 percent receive seven or more. These statistics are slightly different from those mentioned earlier probably because of a different sample. The drugs reported as being used among these older adults are

1. Cardiac/hypertensive drugs (medications for heart disease, high blood pressure, blood vessel diseases), 65 percent.
2. Psychotropic drugs including tranquilizers, sleeping pills, or antidepressants, 33 percent.

3. Gastrointestinal drugs (for ulcers, constipation, colitis, etc), 24 percent.

The Tampa Bay survey (see the Appendix) of older homeless adults provides information on the medication usage pattern among a group of 103 older homeless adults, age 50+ (see also Table 8.2).

Table 8.2
Medication Usage in a Group of Older Homeless Adults
Tampa Bay Area of Florida

Medications	Percentage
Cardiac/hypertensive drugs	20.4%
Psychotropic drugs	10.7%
Anti-inflammatory/pain	9.7%
Respiratory/antihistamine	5.8%
Gastrointestinal	3.9%
Antibiotics	2.9%
Vitamins	2.9%
Hypoglycemics	1.9%
Miscellaneous	1.0%

This pattern is similar to that of housed older adults in order of frequency, although it varies from the homeless adults usage pattern presented earlier. Drugs most frequently taken by this subpopulation of homeless come from completely different medication groups, (i.e., cardiovascular and psychotropic). Bowdler's (1989) homeless adults primarily used medications from the antibiotic and respiratory family. Another interesting finding is the low usage of gastrointestinal drugs, a usage lower than that of homeless adults in general and also lower than that of housed older adults. This is surprising because constipation is recognized as an important problem for older adults. This difference may be the result of oversight on the part of the older homeless adults, the result of an environmental situation which requires a great amount of walking and could foster regularity, or the result of a lack of medical care leading to undertreatment.

Bowdler (1989) does not mention polypharmacy. The Tampa Bay survey shows that 26.5 percent of the 34 older adults on medication took three or more. Since polypharmacy is a frequent phenomenon, the staff member of a service agency must do a complete history of the medication usage for each homeless person. This history should include not only prescribed medications but over-the-counter drugs, those shared or borrowed, street drug usage, and alcohol usage. Unfortunately, alcohol usage is frequently omitted when looking for multiple drug use, although the effects of this legal drug mixed with prescription medications are highly unpredictable and sometimes deadly. This is especially critical for older homeless adults, among whom use of multiple prescriptions is common.

TREATMENT COMPLIANCE ISSUES

Compliance problems exist among the housed population. Failure to follow treatment regimens is reported to cost millions of dollars annually and to diminish productivity and life rewards. This phenomenon is more prevalent in older adults. Half do not take drugs which are prescribed, while one fourth make mistakes serious enough to cause illness. Consequently, older adults represent almost half of drug intoxication cases admitted to hospitals (Butler et al., 1991).

Nyamathi and Schuler (1989) write that "compliance refers to an individual's perceived ability in taking the prescribed medication as ordered" (p. 47). Many variables affect general compliance according to Becker (1984): (1) The individual has to value the goal of the treatment; (2) the individual has to have faith that the goal can be reached; (3) the person thinks that the disease will cause undesirable or unacceptable symptoms; (4) the illness may have a moderately severe impact on some aspects of the person's life; (5) taking the medication for the diagnosed illness may decrease the susceptibility to a more severe physical complication; and, (6) obtaining or taking the medication will not require overcoming barriers such as cost, convenience, pain, or embarrassment.

Additional factors also include "demographic variables and socio-psychological variables such as adjustment to illness, client control of treatment choices, self-concept, social support, and the provider-patient relationship" (Nyamathi & Schuler, 1989).

IMPLICATIONS FOR THE HOMELESS POPULATION

From these general guidelines one can extrapolate some of the difficulties encountered by the homeless population in complying with a medication regimen. It is difficult for a homeless person to value the goal of treatment when there is little attachment to the vague tomorrow, which may be seen as another day of desperation, a struggle not worth the effort (Filardo, 1985). In addition, can the homeless have faith that the goal may be reached when there are so many problems accessing the system and when money is not available in sufficient quantity to buy the medication? Most factors inherent to good compliance are very difficult to follow for the homeless person. Kinchen and Wright (1991) report that the homeless person's overall physical and mental well-being is threatened by more present concerns; basic needs come before prevention and health maintenance.

Throughout several articles, similar factors of noncompliance can be found. Nyamathi and Schuler (1989) prioritize those factors. As agreed among the 61 urban homeless adults they studied, compliance was impeded by, in order of importance, no privacy, no area to store medications, medication stolen, medication lost, and difficulty in getting medications. The authors mention that several homeless adults report forgetting to take medications or having medication stolen during frequent drinking binges. Compliance varied from none to very seldom taking the medication (18 percent), taking it half of the time (13.1 percent), and taking it most of the time or all the time (68.8 percent). One fifth of the homeless adults reported no compliance problem.

The only example provided for lack of privacy was difficult access to bathroom facilities when the person took diuretics (Piantieri, Vicic, Byrd, Brammer, & Michael, 1990). It would be interesting to learn from those who reported privacy as a primary reason for noncompliance what else might have triggered their answer. Privacy seems to have an unusual importance if solely related to the side effects of diuretics (i.e., increased urination). Medications administered through rectal and intravenous routes, and possibly the application of patches, require privacy; however, the frequency of their usage seems too low to bring privacy to a first order of importance. It may be that taking medications is considered a stigma and one does not want to take them in public, whatever the route may be.

Lack of storage leads to several problems. First, it is easier to lose medications if they are kept on the person, and second, there is a greater chance of being assaulted. Third, medication can become useless by becoming wet, dirty, or pulverized by constant rubbing in a pocket or a purse (Piantieri et al., 1990). A further problem is sharing medications, a dangerous practice. Bowdler (1989) writes that several clinic patients who were given acetaminophen with codeine from an emergency room visit were assaulted and badly injured because they possessed a narcotic.

The establishment of a sterile injection site for a homeless diabetic is a problem. Alcohol used for skin cleansing may be ingested or confiscated by others. The possession of hypodermic syringes adds a risk of significant magnitude in the violent homeless environment. Insulin can be rendered unusable and/or lose its potency with the lack of refrigeration during the summer or with freezing temperatures during the winter (Bowdler, 1989). The temperature required to maintain effectiveness is between 30°F and 80°F; therefore, having this medication available on a consistent basis is difficult for the homeless diabetic. Other types of medications can also lose potency when exposed to sunlight, heat, and moisture, an important factor to consider for a homeless person living in a warm climate.

It is difficult for many homeless adults to obtain necessary medications. Piantieri et al. (1990) explain that there are long waits and many hardships in negotiating the system. Kinchen and Wright (1991) add that the cost of medications can be prohibitive for the homeless adult as well as for service providers. Cost is an even greater problem when the medication is taken as a life-long regimen, such as in treatment of hypertension, heart problem, or diabetes. Additionally, the lack of watches and access to clocks make medication schedules a complex, difficult regimen (Bowdler, 1989), especially if more than a daily dose is required. A multidose regimen can be very confusing and impractical for homeless adults.

Other noncompliance factors given by some authors include undesirable side effects, inability to understand recommendations, lack of motivation because of the asymptomatic nature of the disease (Piantieri et al., 1990), behavior problems such as acting out (Ridgely, Osher, & Talbott, 1987), medication viewed as "useless voodoo" because of little improvement in the immediate situation (Filardo, 1985), and lack of monitoring (Levy & Henly, 1985). The list is long enough to support the fact that compliance for homeless adults is very difficult. Without assistance from service providers, a medication regimen can hardly be maintained.

FACTORS IMPEDING COMPLIANCE

In addition to the factors inherent to the homeless environment, older homeless adults may have hearing impairments that affect the understanding of instructions given by the prescribing physician. Others may have difficulty reading small print on the labels where medication name and schedule are written. Without a steady hand, taking liquid medication, opening "child-proof" bottles, or preparing and administering insulin or other injectable medications is not easy. Memory problems can create errors of judgment and confusion. These additional factors can decrease the self-administration capacity of the older homeless adult and may lead to under- or overmedication (Butler et al., 1991).

In the homeless environment, the absence of a strong support system can lead to misunderstanding and decreased opportunity for clarification of instructions. The lack of orientation mechanisms such as calendar, watches, or radio increases confusion and exacerbates the memory loss experienced by some older homeless adults.

INTERVENTIONS TO ENHANCE COMPLIANCE

Existing literature suggests several methods to enhance compliance. Nyamathi and Schuler (1989) report how homeless adults rank factors that helped them take medications as prescribed. In general, compliance is positively correlated to possession of goods, services available, and educational and psychological factors.

Practical ideas to assist compliance include (1) wallet-sized medication card with name, address, and telephone number of the prescribing facility which make dispensing easier (Bowdler, 1989); (2) pillbox with separate slots for hours of the day and days of the week; (3) transdermal patches (good for seven days) to replace daily multidoses, when appropriate and available (Piantieri et al., 1990); (4) a daily single dose, such as time-released medication, instead of multiple doses; and (5) weather-resistant packages (Kinchen & Wright, 1991). Medication taken only once or twice per day has other advantages. It deemphasizes the importance of medication and weakens the message that every problem can be solved with a pill. It also decreases the stigma attached to an illness and helps homeless adults pursue employment with less inconvenience (Levy & Henly, 1985).

Services that could facilitate compliance are numerous. *Morbidity and Mortality Weekly Report* (Centers, 1987) advises that to enhance compliance in treatment of tuberculosis, medications should be taken under the supervision of a responsible person at a shelter or some location convenient to the homeless person. "Although currently recommended regimens specify that medications should be administered daily for the first 1-2 months of treatment, the supervision of daily therapy for homeless out-patients may not be feasible" (Centers, 1987, p. 259). There are two possible alternatives: (1) Provide direct supervision five days per week and ask the client to take the medications on his or her own the other days; and (2) provide direct observation three days a week using higher dosages. This suggestion may be applicable as an alternative pattern for the administration of other medications.

Some homeless adults report that particularly helpful services would include having medications available at service centers, transportation to county facilities where medications are provided, and assistance in accessing the complicated bureaucratic system (Nyamathi & Schuler, 1989). Kinchen and Wright (1991) offer other suggestions. First, services that would help maintain contacts with homeless adults may include scheduling more frequent appointments and writing prescriptions for shorter periods. Second, outreach workers monitoring clients on the streets could enhance compliance. Third, a no-wait, drop-in station for immediate dispensing of medications could attend to all needs at one time through multiple consultation with health-care professionals such as physicians, social workers, dieticians, and counselors.

Education can be instrumental in compliance. Clients must be instructed on possible side effects, appropriate precautions, and ways to avoid medication interactions. They should also be aware that dosage adjustments or changes are possible in order to lessen adverse reactions. Another aspect of education concerns the understanding of personal illness (Bowdler, 1989), its influence on daily activities, and the role of medication in lessening or eliminating these consequences. A well-informed client is more apt to take the steps necessary to follow a medication regimen.

Psychological factors also are important. A trusting relationship between the service provider and the homeless adult allows for a more complete history and a better understanding of the problems leading to noncompliance. Service providers should tailor expectations to the functional level of the client. Kinchen and Wright (1991) add that the providers' perseverance and creativity, individuality, comprehensiveness, flexibility, accessibility, and effective communications are important for continuity of care, and continuity of care is an enhancer of compliance (Nyamathi & Schuler, 1989).

Despite several creative interventions, compliance continues as a major issue. Nyamathi and Schuler (1989) quote Brickner and Kaufman (1973) as saying that only about half of their homeless adult clients kept their clinic appointments or emergency room referrals. We may therefore assume that the recommendation to schedule more frequent appointments may not lead to better compliance unless it is in conjunction with prescriptions that end at the same time as the appointment date. Even that may not help if the homeless person is not close to the clinic at that time and has no transportation. Furthermore, homeless persons do not seek treatment during periods of heavy alcohol abuse (Piantieri et al., 1990).

Another concern is the cost of newer and more effective medications such as patches. Homeless adults and agencies cannot afford them. Therefore, older medications with frequent dosing intervals and side effects are the only ones dispensed (Kinchen & Wright, 1991). Several factors positively related to compliance may not be feasible depending on individual circumstances or funding. But one should exhaust all alternatives and not give up hope, because one client differs from another.

DRUG SIDE EFFECTS, INTERACTIONS, AND PRECAUTIONS

Butler et al. (1991) write about another aspect of medication therapy. They state that drug reactions probably occur in 3 to 9 percent of younger adults. This risk is about 33 percent greater in those aged 50 to 59 than in people aged 40 to 49, and the risk increases as people age (Wolfe & Hope, 1993). These reactions can range from not very serious to serious injury, to hospitalization, and even to death. It is important to recognize these side effects in order to make appropriate decisions regarding the homeless medication regimen.

The most serious adverse reactions in older adults occur with the use of tranquilizers, sleeping pills, and other drugs that affect the mind; next, with cardiovascular drugs such as high blood pressure drugs, digoxin, and drugs for abnormal heart rate; and then with drugs used for treating gastrointestinal problems (Wolfe & Hope, 1993). An example of such side effects is the sudden onset of confusion following the ingestion of Valium. Another is a decrease in sexual function when one takes Lopressor, a medication to lower blood pressure. A person treated for gastric ulcers with Tagamet may experience depressive symptoms. Almost any type of medication has a potential for multiple side effects.

Older homeless adults face more problems because of the frequency of polypharmacy. A medication regimen including several drugs increases the risk of side effects. For example, a client with a heart problem may take a heart medication and a water pill, both of which may cause confusion, depression, loss of appetite, nausea, vomiting, and/or hallucinations. If one more drug is added to this combination, the extent of the possible reactions can be multiplied. On the other hand, the combination of two or more drugs may lessen or even eliminate the effectiveness of one of the drugs taken. For example, taking an antacid (Tums) decreases the effect of an antibiotic (tetracycline) unless the drugs are taken three hours apart. This makes it very difficult to evaluate which drug is creating the problem.

The use of medication usually entails precautions which may vary between drug classifications and also within medications in the same classification. Certain cardiac/hypertensive drugs should be taken with food or milk and require a diet rich in potassium, adequate in magnesium, and low in salt. Others require monitoring of pulse, periodic blood pressure checks, and/or blood testing. Most of the time alcohol use is to be avoided.

Anti-inflammatory and pain medications require intake of food or water and periodic blood tests. These drugs may also increase sensitivity to sunlight. Several may lead to some level of drug addiction; thus, discontinuation cannot be sudden. Tylenol, a frequently used over-the-counter drug, cannot be exposed to moisture or strong light. Some of these drugs when taken with an anticoagulant or a painkiller can create undesirable, even dangerous side effects. Some gastrointestinal drugs (e.g., antacids) must be taken with plenty of fluids and ingested at least one hour before eating. Exposure to sun when taking some types of gastrointestinal drugs can result in skin rash. In addition, respiratory medications and antihistamines have to be taken with food or milk, and alcohol should be avoided.

It is important to take the full course of antibiotic therapy to obtain the desired effects. These medications increase sensitivity to sun exposure. Some antibiotics need to be taken with food, while others should be taken on an empty stomach, and several require abstinence from alcohol. Periodic lab testing may be needed to evaluate therapeutic blood levels.

Hypoglycemics require frequent dosage adjustments depending on food intake, activity, and sickness. They are used on a long-range basis, and treatment becomes expensive. The client should have some form of sugar available at all times, and alcohol should be avoided. Regular check-ups and lab tests are recommended to obtain maximum control. Low blood sugar symptoms may mimic alcohol intoxication.

Vitamins and minerals need to be taken with food other than milk or milk products. When one takes cortisone, the diet should be low in salt, potassium, protein, and folic acid. This medication cannot be stopped abruptly, and periodic blood tests are necessary to evaluate side effects, one of which is anemia. Hormones have to be taken with food, and smoking and sun exposure should be avoided.

Many precautions cannot be followed on a consistent basis by the homeless adult population. Exposure to sunlight, which may be difficult to avoid, creates a problem that is unlikely to occur among the general population. Maintaining a proper diet is almost impossible in an environment where food is hardly available. When available, choices are minimal and may not be those that will prevent adverse medication reactions. Food or water may also be difficult to obtain at the time the medication is to be taken.

Another problem more prevalent among the homeless adults than in the general population is alcohol use. Ropers and Boyer (1987) report that 64 percent of a group of 269 homeless adults from Los Angeles sometimes drink. Among those drinking, 55 percent did not exhibit symptoms of alcoholism, 25 percent were abusers, and 19 percent were alcohol dependent. The homeless client is, therefore, at increased risk for medication reactions. Bouts of alcohol consumption lead to poor water intake and increased diuretic effect. Significant volume depletion ensues, complicating the use of diuretics (Piantieri et al., 1990). The stereotyping of homeless as alcoholics places the homeless diabetic at greater risk for being put in jail instead of being treated (e.g., an insulin reaction may be confused with a state of inebriation). Another issue is related to the high content of alcohol in some medications. They may be used to satisfy the cravings of homeless alcoholics, or they may increase the frequency of crime perpetuated against those who possess them.

Butler et al. (1991) write that older people absorb, distribute, and excrete drugs differently from younger adults. The absorption rate is often slower because of reduced blood flow in the liver. This slow absorption lengthens the time course and duration of drug effects. Drugs are also distributed differently. There is a relatively greater accumulation in the older adult's body fat than in the younger adult's body fat. Slow excretion may occur when there is kidney impairment. Because of these changes, drug sensitivity is assumed to be increased. As a consequence, the principle of drug management for the elderly emphasizes a 30 to 50 percent decrease from the dosage usually prescribed for younger adults. This smaller amount is usually more effective. Unfortunately, this is not common practice in the medical field because "medical and nursing education does not yet focus adequately on pharmacology and clinical pharmacy as it relates to old age" (Butler et al., 1991, p. 446). Therefore, the older homeless adult may suffer many reactions, and most will be misinterpreted as normal or expected changes of aging.

SUMMARY

Medication is always an issue for homeless adults and even more so for older homeless adults. Their medication patterns are different, drug compliance is rendered difficult because of their environment, and side effects may be more likely to occur from inappropriate use. Medication side effects and interactions are a greater risk for older homeless adults, whose age group is known for polypharmacy and altered reactions to medication.

When an older homeless adult reports symptoms of medication reactions, the service provider must eliminate the possibility of malnutrition, alcoholism, and drug abuse, conditions which are likely to cause similar symptoms. Medication side effects may also be mistaken for normal manifestations of aging, especially when confusion and loss of memory are present. It is important to differentiate between side effects and physical or psychological conditions such as depression, dementia, or delirium. One cannot assume that symptoms observed are directly associated with medications.

The medication regimen for older homeless adults is a challenge to service providers. They must gain the confidence of the older adults in order to obtain a complete history and evaluate their current situation. Service providers may also become agents of change and modify the environment to facilitate compliance. Finally, they have to overcome system barriers in order to obtain proper referrals for medical treatment.

REFERENCES

Becker, M. (1984). *The health belief model and personal health behavior.* Thorofare, NJ: Charles B. Slack.

Bowdler, J. R. (1989). Health problems of the homeless in America. *Nurse Practitioner, 14*(7), 44-51.

Butler, N., Lewis, M., & Sunderland, T. (1991). *Aging and mental health: Positive psychosocial and biomedical approaches* (4th ed.). New York: Macmillan.

Centers for Disease Control, Division of Tuberculosis Control. (1987). Tuberculosis control among homeless populations. *Morbidity and Mortality Weekly Report*, *36*(17), 257-260.

Filardo, T. (1985). Chronic disease management in the homeless. In P.W. Brickner, L. K. Scharer, B. Conanan, A. Elvy, & M. Savarese (Eds.), *Health care of homeless people* (pp. 19-31). New York: Springer-Verlag.

Hillsborough County Board of Commissioners, Department of Community Services and Planning. (1990). *Hillsborough County's comprehensive homeless assistance plan (CHAP)* (Publication No. 90-1311). Tampa, FL: Department of Community Services and Planning.

Kinchen, K., & Wright, J. D. (1991). Hypertension management in health care for the homeless clinics. Results from a survey. *American Journal of Public Health, 81*(9), 1163-1165.

Kutza, E. A., & Keigher, S. M. (1991). The elderly "new homeless": An emerging population at risk. *Social Work, 36*(4), 288-293.

Levy, L. T., & Henly, B. (1985). Psychiatric care of the homeless: Human beings or cases? In P. W. Brickner, L. K., Scharer, B., Conanan, A., Elvy, & M. Savarese (Eds.), *Health care of homeless people* (pp. 205-219). New York: Springer-Verlag.

Nyamathi, A., & Schuler, P. (1989). Factors affecting prescribed medication compliance of the urban homeless adult. *Nurse Practitioner, 14*(8), 47-54.

Piantieri, O., Vicic, W., Byrd, R., Brammer, S. Michael, M. (1990). Hypertension screening and treatment in the homeless. In P. W. Brickner, L. K. Scharer, B. Conanan, M. Savarese, & B. C. Scanlan (Eds.), *Under the safety net: The health and social welfare of the homeless in the United States* (pp. 250-262). New York: W. W. Norton.

Ridgely, M., Osher, F. C., & Talbott, J. A. (1987). *Chronic mentally ill young adults with substance abuse problems: Treatment and training issues*. Unpublished manuscript. University of Maryland, School of Medicine, Mental Health Policy Studies, Department of Psychiatry.

Ropers, R. H., & Boyer, R. (Spring 1987). Homelessness as a health risk. *Alcohol Health & Research World, 11*(3), 38-41, 89.

Solomon, F., White, C. C., Parron, D. C., & Mendelson, W. B. (1979). Sleeping pills, insomnia and medical practice. *New England Journal of Medicine, 300*, 803-808.

U. S. Department of Housing and Urban Development. (1984). *A report to the secretary on homeless and emergency shelters*. Washington, DC: U.S. Government Printing Office.

Wolfe, S. M., & Hope, R. (1993). *Worst pills, best pills II*. Washington, DC: Public Citizen Health Research Group.

9

Psychotropic Medications

Louisette A. Boucher

Psychotropic medications are prescribed to effect change in thinking, mood, behavior, and mental activity. They are grouped differently according to authors and the following categories were selected for this review: (1) antidepressant, (2) antipsychotic, (3) antianxiety, (4) antiparkinsonian, (5) anticonvulsant, and (6) psychostimulant. Definitions and therapeutic effects of each category will be discussed.

Butler, Lewis, and Sunderland (1991) write that patients and their physicians often see these drugs as "crutches" that may "suppress" the symptom but do not address the underlying psychological problem. The general purpose of these drugs is to aid the management of mental illnesses by controlling symptoms. Their therapeutic effects permit mentally ill persons to function more normally and give attention to problems other than the symptoms of their illness. Clients are calmed, concentration is facilitated, distorted thoughts are decreased, anxiety is reduced, and mood is elevated. As a consequence, clients are more comfortable in the company of others, are more confident about their perceptions, and feel less threatened with regard to success and survival (Long & Jacobs, 1986). Crockett and Kunkel (1989) believe that these drugs can help some clients benefit from other therapeutic approaches such as psychotherapy, behavior modification, and rehabilitation therapy.

Once the medications have produced the expected therapeutic effects, clients need to adjust their expectations to their new situation (i.e., become rehabilitated). They need to develop skills such as acquiring self-discipline, making choices, maintaining social relationships, and organizing their lives (Long & Jacobs, 1986). One problem often encountered during the course of a psychotropic regimen is side effects. Some of these undesired results are temporary while others may require a change in medication dosage or in the medication itself. The service provider should be able to inform the client about these disturbing symptoms and about the possible use of alternative drugs to which clients may respond more favorably. Information follows on the usage pattern in older homeless adults, compliance issues and interventions related to the mentally ill homeless, and therapeutic effects for each category of psychotropic drugs.

PSYCHOTROPIC USAGE PATTERNS

Literature is scarce on the subject of psychotropic drug use in the homeless population. Bowdler (1989) discusses usage patterns, stating that 12 percent of 77 homeless adults seen at a primary clinic in Richmond, Virginia, used neuroleptic and tranquilizer drugs. The Tampa Bay survey of older homeless adults reveals a 10.7 percent usage; more specifically, 11 of the 103 participants used some type of psychotropic drugs (see the Appendix). This is a much lower rate than the 33 percent seen in the housed older adult population, as reported by Wolfe and Hope (1993).

One wonders if the difficulty in obtaining medications is one factor that could explain this lower usage pattern. An interesting area of research would be a study of the usage pattern of older homeless veterans, who may have better access to medications, in order to learn whether their usage is closer to that of the housed older adult population. The sedative action of these drugs may also lead to lower usage among the homeless. Persons living on the street must be on constant alert to avoid assault and robbery. This alertness would be negatively affected by any of the psychotropic drugs.

COMPLIANCE ISSUES IN THE HOMELESS MENTALLY ILL

While there are general compliance issues, there are issues specific to mentally ill homeless adults. A major barrier to psychiatric treatment is the failure to take prescribed medications. Between one third and one half of psychiatric outpatients take less medication than prescribed (Dow, 1989).

Some factors of noncompliance in the mentally ill are described by Crockett and Kunkel (1989), who state that depressed persons may feel unworthy of getting better or of receiving free medications. They also mention that paranoid clients may believe that someone is trying to poison them with the drug. Others may believe it is a sign of illness to take medications, or they may equate medications with punishment or addiction.

In the best of circumstances, a confused client sometimes cannot follow a complex medication schedule even with the help of family members or home health workers. Mentally ill homeless adults live in a disorganized environment without adequate social support. As a result, a simple medication regimen can become a complicated task (Filardo, 1985). Among his many clients who are on anticonvulsant therapy, Crane (1985) reports that "compliance with Dilantin, phenobarbital, or Tegretol regimen is unpredictable and is complicated by alcohol consumption" (p. 313).

Continuity of care is important to compliance. If medications prescribed vary from one service center to another, the mentally ill person may become disillusioned and confused. This can lead to a lack of faith in the mental health care system. As a result, clients will probably be seen only occasionally when brought to an emergency room or stabilization center. Effective treatment and compliance will both be jeopardized by such limited contacts (Dow, 1989).

As mentioned earlier, survival on the streets requires the individual to remain alert. When medications produce sedation in early or late evening, a time when clues to orientation are decreased and when alertness is needed for protection, the situation may become troublesome, if not dangerous. Consequently, mentally ill homeless adults may decide to discontinue medications even if they are necessary to maintain a normal level of functioning.

ENHANCING COMPLIANCE

In addition to interventions useful for compliance with other types of medications, Dow (1989) discusses the possible use of long-acting injectable versions of major tranquilizers. He recommends a periodic count of medications during appointment visits, a practice that has been known to increase compliance. Recommendations include the assessment of the client's daily habits and subsequent adaptation of the medication schedule to the most appropriate daily events. For example, Dow writes that "a substance-abusing individual who often drinks alcohol in the evening should not be told to take medications at bedtime" (p. 131). If someone regularly visits a drop-in center, attends a day program, or eats at a soup kitchen, the service provider should advise that person to associate medication times with these activities.

Another simple intervention is asking clients whether they take their medications routinely. This helpful tool, not used often enough, can reveal compliance problems and may emphasize the importance of the medication regimen. Another helpful intervention is the use of cognitive approaches to modify negative beliefs. Such approaches include a dialogue where the clients argue against their own thoughts, a contract to take medications, and the discussion of long-term versus short-term benefits of the medications. It is important for clients to understand that it is reasonable to discuss concerns about medications and to attempt to solve as many problems as possible. When side effects are openly reported and discussed, they may be reduced or eliminated by simply decreasing the dosage or changing the medication.

There are some simple recommendations for common side effects that service providers can offer clients. Sugarless gum or sugarless candies relieve dry mouth, but clients should be advised to avoid sugar-containing products that can increase the risk of dental caries. Bulk laxatives such as Metamucil or Fiberall relieve constipation. Clients, especially older adults, should be cautioned about orthostatic hypotension (the sudden drop in blood pressure when one gets up). This causes dizziness and significantly increases the risk of hip fracture in older adults because of the possibility of a secondary fall. Clients should be instructed to get up slowly and to sit down immediately if they become dizzy. A diet low in fat and carbohydrates and an increase in exercise should be suggested to prevent weight gain. Finally, clients should be referred to a physician for treatment of blurred vision, urinary retention, sexual dysfunction, or neurological side effects (Kaplan & Sadock, 1991).

PSYCHOTROPIC CLASSIFICATIONS

Antidepressant drugs are used to manage major depression and the accompanying anxiety and tension. Wolfe and Hope (1993) write that fewer than 1 percent of older adults are diagnosed with major depression. The authors add that 37 percent of the antidepressant drugs are prescribed to older adults who make up only one sixth of the population. Overtreatment, they add, may be related to the failure to diagnose drug-induced depression. Butler et al. (1991) believe that this overtreatment reflects "the anxiety of doctors and other health personnel, their impatience with older people (to whom they often rather give a pill than listen), and their own need for instant gratification (treatment results)" (p. 446).

Depression in older adults is a significant concern. Estimates of depression vary greatly and one wonders if older adults are not underdiagnosed because of their tendency to discuss psychological symptoms in somatic terms, a result of their socialization or stigma of mental illness. Another concern is the refractory nature of true depression in older adults when not treated appropriately. As noted by Schaie and Willis (1991), older adults may be quite depressed, but not enough so to meet all the criteria in the *Diagnostic and Statistical Manual-III-R*. The authors add that when studies rely on screening scales to determine the presence of depressive symptoms, they show increased symptoms, particularly over the age of 70.

Identifying depression is important, because it responds well to treatment and quality of life is enhanced. When drug therapy is selected, clients should be instructed that therapeutic effects are not immediate. If results are unsatisfactory after at least four weeks of treatment with careful management, changing medication can be considered (Kaplan & Sadock, 1991). Clients should also be advised of the side effects of the medication. Seven to 35 percent of older depressed adults suffer from antidepressant-related confusional episodes compared to fewer than 1 percent of younger adults. This is the result of increased sensitivity to the effects of anticholinergic medications (Butler et al., 1991). Other side effects, as reported by De Vane (1990), include the aggravation of some types of glaucoma and some cases of paralytic ileus. Kaplan and Sadock (1991) warn that alcohol, hypnotic medications, over-the-counter cold medications, and aspirin increase the antidepressant effects while cigarette smoking decreases the plasma effect. These side effects are relevant issues for older homeless adults who may not have the necessary social supports to obtain adequate warnings.

Butler et al. (1991) report that the outcome of treatment with another type of antidepressant, monoamine oxidase inhibitors (MAO) such as Nardil and Parnate, depends on appropriate education, supervision, and proper diet. Kaplan and Sadock (1991) warn that these drugs should be used cautiously in clients with hypertension. The authors add that when the drug is ingested with food high in thiamine, it may lead to hypertensive crisis, which can be life threatening. De Vane (1990) recommends specific dietary restrictions. Those pertinent to homeless adults would be red wine, gin, vodka, whiskey, pizza, beef or chicken liver, soy sauce, packaged soups, pickled or smoked food such as pepperoni, dry sausage, and pickled fish. Kaplan and Sadock (1991) note that bee stings may also cause hypertensive crisis. These restrictions are difficult to control in the homeless environment. Although the incidence of alcohol use is not as high in homeless adults age 50+ as in younger adults, it remains a concern when MAO inhibitors are prescribed. Because of the limited food choices, the danger of side effects may be increased.

Lithium carbonate is prescribed for manic-depressive illnesses and cyclic depression. The toxic dose is close to the therapeutic level, making accurate management and periodic blood tests a must (De Vane, 1990). In *Drug Information for the Health Care Professional* (United States, 1994), it is noted that concurrent use with diuretics; large amounts of coffee, tea, or colas, and severe dehydration increase the risk of toxicity. Hypothyroidism may also be induced in predisposed older adults. Drinking two to three quarts of water each day and storing the medication away from direct light and heat or damp places is recommended. In an environment where the homeless person has little control over exposure to high temperatures, the sodium lost through increased perspiration may place the person at greater risk. Furthermore, older adults are often advised to lower the amount of sodium in their diet or are given diuretics. Both of these situations make it more difficult to maintain a normal sodium blood level, leading to a more severe and unpredictable course of lithium toxicity.

Antipsychotic medications are also known as neuroleptics or major tranquilizers. They are mainly prescribed for schizophrenic disorders (De Vane, 1990) but are also prescribed for other mental health disorders, including manifestations of agitation and psychosis (Kaplan & Sadock, 1991). The therapeutic effects only produce an incomplete reduction of symptoms. Symptoms such as combativeness, hyperactivity, tension, hostility, hallucinations, delusion, and sociability respond well, but symptoms such as insight, judgment, and memory are not likely to respond well (De Vane, 1990). Individuals regain a functional level that gives them a seminormal life and permits them to remain in society. They are still impaired, often are unable to find or hold a job, and have difficulty living with others. Consequently, as Kaplan and Sadock (1991) remark, the lack of planning for follow-up outpatient treatment has led to a homeless problem among these individuals.

Wolfe and Hope (1993) write that individuals under age 60 receive four antipsychotic prescriptions a year, while those age 60+ receive 10. Often these drugs are unnecessarily prescribed for recent onset of hallucination or delirium that is drug induced or related to alcohol or drug withdrawal. In more than 80 percent of the cases, these drugs are prescribed to control disturbances in older demented persons or to treat sleep disorders and chronic anxiety, a blatant misuse according to the authors.

With high dosage, side effects are unavoidable, especially because older adults are more sensitive to these drugs. Many clients who have experienced side effects of these drugs refuse further therapy (Crockett & Kunkel, 1989). The most worrisome effect is tardive dyskinesia, the slow and involuntary movement of the tongue, lips, arms, and other body parts (Butler et al., 1991). If this develops, Gomez and Gomez (1990) recommend reducing the dose or prescribing another type of antipsychotic rather than adding an antiparkinsonian, which could lead to additional complications.

Because photosensitivity is a side effect, clients should be advised not to spend more than 30 to 60 minutes in the sun and to use sunscreen (Kaplan & Sadock, 1991). This is difficult for homeless people. Some of these drugs also impair body temperature regulation and decrease perspiration. To decrease the possibility of heat stroke, clients should avoid high temperature and humidity, which is also difficult for homeless people. Older adults are particularly prone to the hypotensive effect and confusional state associated with these drugs. They require smaller dosage and closer monitoring (De Vane, 1990). The therapeutic effect in older adults may take longer than four weeks, although it lasts long after cessation of the regimen. This can diminish the patient's incentive to comply with a regular schedule and makes it more difficult to determine whether the client is compliant.

Antianxiety medications help fearful and tense people relax. They are generally called tranquilizers by the public, while psychiatrists call them minor tranquilizers, anxiolytics or hypnotics (Long & Jacobs, 1986).

Sedative and hypnotic drugs overlap with antianxiety drugs. They are used for insomnia, muscle relaxation, and sedation but are also used to relieve anxiety (Crockett & Kunkel, 1989). These medications usually provide quick therapeutic results but are habit forming and often may be taken in increasingly larger doses to maintain consistent effects. A sudden discontinuation leads to withdrawal symptoms which can sometimes be lethal.

Wolfe and Hope (1993) report on the overuse of these drugs by older adults and usage over a longer period of time. These drugs are often prescribed for complaints of insomnia without obtaining a careful history of the problem. Older patients may not have true insomnia. Their sleep may be interrupted at night, but their sleep-wake cycle over a period of 24 hours still provides them with the required seven to nine hours of sleep (Butler et al., 1991). Education would be more appropriate in these cases than medication.

If these medications are not properly fitted to client needs, they may provide sedation and muscle relaxation that are not welcomed by the homeless person who needs the ability to be aroused easily. On the other hand, older homeless adults may become abusers or sell or trade these drugs. Because of the high potential for abuse, the service provider needs to be alert to signs of hoarding.

Valium and Librium are often problematic for older adults because they may produce delirium. Other drugs may cause or increase sleep apnea, a condition in which breathing stops for a varying length of time while one sleeps. As a result of the decrease in respiration rate, sleep apnea can be threatening for an older adult with severe lung disease (Wolfe & Hope, 1993). Many over-the-counter drugs, such as Sominex, Nytol, and Sleep-Eze, contain unsafe levels of antihistamine and may also contain a medication that can cause outbursts of uncontrollable behavior in older adults (Butler et al., 1991).

De Vane (1990) writes that antiparkinsonian drugs are used to treat Parkinson's disease, drug-induced parkinsonian symptoms, and psychoactive drug withdrawal symptoms. In 51 percent of older adults, the symptoms are drug induced, according to Wolfe and Hope (1993). The authors recommend evaluating the drug regimen, discontinuing the drug if misused, decreasing dosage, or prescribing an alternative drug with less adverse effects. De Vane (1990) mentions that clozapine (Clozaril or Leponex) may be the only antipsychotic that does not produce parkinsonian symptoms. The author also adds that when antiparkinsonians are used with over-the-counter antihistamines with atropine-like properties, a toxic syndrome can result. Age also increases toxicity risks. Less severe adverse side effects include dry mouth, blurred vision, worsening of glaucoma, decreased perspiration, and increased body temperature (Wolfe & Hope, 1993). One can conclude that older homeless adults are at great risk for toxicity and heat stroke.

Anticonvulsant drugs are not psychotropics but are included in the classification because they are often used by mentally ill clients for the control of epileptic seizures. Frequent blood levels are necessary to maintain proper therapeutic benefits and to avoid adverse reactions (Crockett & Kunkel, 1989). Side effects include easy bruising and skin rashes. The older homeless adult who may not be able to maintain proper dental care or be scheduled for dentist visits, may develop enlarged and tender gums, a serious side effect. The manual *Drug Information for the Health Care Professional* (United States, 1994) reports that when diazepam is taken with erythromycin (antibiotic), the drug level of the anticonvulsant is sharply increased, leading to signs of toxicity. These signs include nausea, vomiting, disturbed balance, and pronounced drowsiness. If the drug is given at the same time as isoniazid (antibiotic for tuberculosis), altered clinical or enhanced adverse effects may result. De Vane (1990) warns that a dosage adjustment may be required. Phenobarbital is often prescribed as an anticonvulsant and may become a feasible substitute when street drugs are unavailable. The nature of the drug increases the risk of being robbed and physically harmed.

Psychostimulant drugs "restore optimism and alertness, elevate mood, increase confidence, power of concentration, willingness to work, and verbal interaction" (Crockett & Kunkel, 1989, p. 126). Prescribing them for older adults remains controversial, according to Butler et al. (1991), who write that these medications should be used only when the older adult cannot tolerate traditional antidepressant treatment and when other approaches have been exhausted. Caffeine is a well-known natural nervous system stimulant and amphetamines and cocaine are psychostimulant drugs that can produce paranoid symptoms.

IMPORTANT ISSUES RELATED TO HOMELESSNESS

Goldfrank (1985) discusses the thermoregulation effects of drugs. Drugs of abuse such as PCP, amphetamines, methadone, heroin, hypnotics, and prescribed psychotropic drugs dramatically affect the ability to perceive and respond appropriately to thermal environmental stress. These drugs alter the central and peripheral nervous systems and have a direct effect on muscles, sweat glands, and blood vessels.

Psychostimulant drugs are associated with increased heat production by muscles and a decrease in perspiration. They can impair circulation, a condition already altered in many older adults. Antipsychotic medications can lead to dramatic temperature shifts and may decrease shivering and thus decrease heat production. The anticholinergic effects of many of these drugs lead to a loss of body heat evaporation.

Thermoregulation effects can have dramatic consequences. Toxins of abuse "usually enhance the risks of exposure to environmental extremes," according to Goldfrank (1985, p. 61), because of decreased perception of the environment. Older homeless adults may perceive the degree of heat inaccurately. They may absorb heat from the environment during the summer, or they may lose heat to the environment during the winter. The result may be increased frequency of heat stroke or its opposite, hypothermia. Impaired circulation and decreased blood supply to extremities may result in cold injury. Because homeless persons have difficulty accessing medical care, when these problems are finally brought to the attention of medical professionals it may be too late for remedial care and amputation may be the only solution.

When any psychotropic drug is taken, the subject of accidental and intentional poisoning becomes an issue. Woolf, Fish, Azzara, and Dean (1990) conclude that older adults are at higher risk for serious poisoning for several reasons. They take multiple medications; they have underlying heart, liver, kidney, or lung disease that can complicate an overdose; age-related physiological changes render them more fragile to toxic effects of medication; confusion, failing eyesight, and memory can be responsible for dosage errors or duplication; and depression may lead to voluntary overdose. Vulnerability and intentionality are important factors to consider.

In addition to age-related factors, service providers must weigh factors associated with mental health disorders. Kaplan and Sadock (1991) discuss several important indicators of suicidal risk. The rate of suicide is high in the first three months after hospital discharge. Two groups are known to be at high risk--clients with depressive disorders, schizophrenia, and substance abuse and clients who frequently visit emergency rooms. Clients with depressive disorders commit suicide more frequently during the early course of the illness. Risk is higher among middle-aged and older adults who are separated, divorced, widowed, or recently bereaved and who are socially isolated. Suicide in clients with schizophrenia tends to be among the relatively young. Alcoholics with an antisocial personality disorder are more likely to commit suicide. Alcoholics who committed suicide were in a depressed mood or had experienced the loss of a close relationship. If a client has attempted suicide previously, the client is a greater risk for a successful suicidal attempt.

Added to age and mental disorder is the state of homelessness. When despair and homelessness make the homeless life seem not worth living, other risk factors are amplified. As a homeless person, physiological changes of aging are accelerated and one may conclude that toxic effects may be experienced before the person is considered an older adult. Life on the street also provides easy access to drugs. These added factors can lead to serious intentional poisoning.

If one adds to these multiple factors the tendency to overprescribe or misprescribe, chances of accidental or intentional poisoning are even greater. Wolfe and Hope (1993) believe that tendencies come from the failure of pharmaceutical companies to provide geriatric information and from physicians' belief that ending a visit by writing a prescription is their accepted role. These tendencies are important when we look at agents of accidental and intentional poisoning. According to Woolf et al. (1990), accidental poisoning in older adult males and females in Massachusetts is mostly from drugs. Although drugs are the major agent of intentional suicide in women, carbon monoxide is the major agent of intentional suicide in men. Klein-Schwartz and Oderda (1991) found that psychotropic drugs, cardiovascular drugs, analgesics and anti-inflammatory drugs, oral hypoglycemics, and theophylline were the drugs most often responsible for poisoning in older adults. In the general population, as reported by Stein, Bonanno, O'Sullivan, and Wachtel (1993), the trend is to use sedative-hypnotics and antidepressants as suicidal agents. Butler et al. (1991) write that alcohol mixed with drugs accounts for approximately 20 percent of drug-related accidental or suicidal deaths per year.

Among psychotropic drugs, benzodiazepine, an anxiolytic that includes Valium, Librium, and Dalmane, is frequently seen in poisoning cases. A review of drug overdoses at Rhode Island Hospital revealed that benzodiazepine was used by nearly one fourth of the individuals in 1979 and 1989; this rate surpassed that of barbiturates. The combination of two drugs and the use of alcohol and one drug also appeared common (Stein et al., 1993). Benzodiazepine can produce significant toxicity when used over a long period of time or when combined with alcohol, an antipsychotic drug, or an antidepressant drug. This combination is more likely to lead to death from respiratory failure (Kaplan & Sadock, 1991; Klein-Schwartz & Oderda, 1991). These medications have been reported to produce inhibition, paradoxical aggression, and suicide attempts and carry a warning in the United Kingdom (Montgomery, 1992).

Tricyclic and tetracyclic antidepressants are increasingly prescribed and have been seen in an increasing proportion of overdoses. These drugs cause frequent and severe cardiovascular and neurological toxic symptoms. Individuals who have cardiovascular disease are at more risk for severe reactions. An overdose is very serious and often fatal. Amoxapine overdose is frequently complicated by renal failure, and death is more likely to result (De Vane, 1990; Kaplan & Sadock, 1991; Klein-Schwartz & Oderda, 1991).

Barbiturates are often the cause of lethal accidents. They are frequently taken with suicidal intent. The combination with alcohol is particularly dangerous and can lead to respiratory arrest, cardiac failure, and death. The lethal dose varies according to acquired tolerance, route of administration, and the excitability of the nervous system (Kaplan & Sadock, 1991).

The nonpsychotic drugs that often are the cause of poisoning include digoxin and aspirin (salicylates). Digoxin causes chronic and acute intoxication, which can lead to ventricular arrhythmias and heart block. Older adults are more apt to develop chronic intoxication to salicylates, which can result in pulmonary edema. Service providers should be aware that neurological abnormalities or breathing difficulties are often a sign of salicylate poisoning (Klein-Schwartz & Oderda, 1991).

To prevent accidental or intentional poisoning, it is best to give a nonrefillable prescription for only a one-week supply of medication. Service providers should be aware of the possibility of hoarding. Direct questions and requests that all medications be brought to each visit may deter hoarding. The most dangerous periods for poisoning are when the medication is still not therapeutically effective and when the individual is beginning to improve. It is a good practice to keep activated charcoal on hand since it is considered the safest emergency treatment for an overdose of any of these drugs. Service providers should always consider poisoning as an emergency situation.

SUMMARY

It is hardly possible for a person living on the street to maintain a planned schedule of psychotropic medication. It is not reasonable to expect that instructions to take medication regularly will be successfully followed, even if the client is cooperative. The homeless environment does not reinforce taking medications and does not offer opportunities for a well-balanced diet or protected sleep. The regimen is doomed to failure unless clients receive support from service providers. The front-line service provider has the best opportunity to provide education on side effects and precautions. This can be done by keeping updated referral manuals at the service center and maintaining a network of physicians or nurses that may be called.

Service providers have the advantage of seeing clients more frequently than medical or nursing professionals and may be the best social support for mentally ill homeless adults. The support they offer can include storage of medications, assistance in taking prescribed drugs, discussion about side effects which might lead clients to noncompliance, recommendations to alleviate some side effects, and referral to physicians when medication adjustment appears necessary or side effects are deemed potentially dangerous.

Close relationships with clients can alert the service provider to potentially dangerous medication abuse or side effects. With a thorough history, careful observation, inquisitive attitude, and timely referral, service providers can help prevent more side effects than would the efforts of a physician or a nurse.

REFERENCES

Bowdler, J. E. (1989). Health problems of the homeless in America. *Nurse Practitioner, 14*(7), 44-51.

Butler, N., Lewis, N., & Sunderland, T. (1991). *Aging and mental health: Positive psychosocial and biomedical approaches* (4th ed.). New York: MacMillan.

Crane, J. (1985). Springfield, Massachusetts: The Sisters of Providence health care for the homeless program. In P. W. Brickner, L. K. Scharer, B. Conanan, A. Elvy, & M. Savarese (Eds.) *Health care of homeless people* (pp. 311-322). New York: Springer-Verlag.

Crockett, B., & Kunkel, M. (1989). Medications used for mental illness. In T.L. Boaz & M. Kunkel (Eds.), *Working with the homeless mentally ill: A resource manual for caregivers* (pp. 109-127). Tampa, FL: University of South Florida, Florida Mental Health Institute.

De Vane, C. L. (1990). *Fundamentals of monitoring psychoactive drug therapy*. Baltimore, MD: Williams & Wilkins.

Dow, M. G. (1989). The problem of psychiatric medication noncompliance with the homeless mentally ill. In T. L. Boaz & M. Kunkel (Eds.), *Working with the homeless mentally ill: A resource manual for caregivers* (pp. 128-134). Tampa, FL: University of South Florida, Florida Mental Health Institute.

Filardo, T. (1985). Chronic disease management in the homeless. In P. W. Brickner, L. K. Scharer, B. Conanan, A. Elvy, & M. Savarese (Eds.), *Health care of homeless people* (pp. 19-31). New York: Springer-Verlag.

Goldfrank, L. (1985). Exposure: Thermoregulatory disorders in the homeless patient. In P. W. Brickner, L. K. Scharer, B. Conanan, A. Elvy, & M. Savarese (Eds.), *Health care of homeless people* (pp. 57-75). New York: Springer-Verlag.

Gomez, G. E., & Gomez, E. A. (1990). The special concerns of neuroleptic use in the elderly. *Journal of Psychosocial Nursing, 28*(1), 7-14.

Kaplan, H. I., & Sadock, B. J. (1991). *Synopsis of psychiatry* (6th ed.). Baltimore, MD: Williams & Wilkins.

Klein-Schwartz, W., & Oderda, G. M. (1991). Poisoning in the elderly. Epidemiological, clinical and management considerations. *Drugs & Aging, 1*(1), 67-89.

Long, A. L., & Jacobs, E. L. (1986). *A curriculum for working with the homeless mentally ill*. Rockville, MD: Division of Education and Service Systems Liason, National Institute of Mental Health.

Montgomery, S. A. (1992). Suicide and antidepressants. *Drugs, 43*(suppl. 2), 24-31.

Schaie, K. W., & Willis, S. L. (1991). *Adult development and aging* (3rd ed.). New York: HarperCollins.

Stein, M. D., Bonanno, J., O'Sullivan, P. S., & Wachtel, T. J. (1993). Changes in the pattern of drug overdoses. *Journal of General Internal Medicine, 8*, 179-184.

United States Pharmacopeial Convention, Inc. (1994). *Drug information for the health care professional* (14th ed.). Taunton, MA: Rand McNally.

Wolfe, S. M., & Hope, R. (1993). *Worst pills, best pills II.* Washington, DC: Public Citizens Health Research Group.

Woolf, A., Fish, S., Azzara, C., & Dean, D. (1990). Serious poisoning among older adults: A study of hospitalization and mortality rates in Massachusetts 1983-85. *American Journal of Public Health, 80*(7), 867-868.

10

Outreach and Empowerment

Judith Sullivan-Mintz

Establishing contact and creating relationships with those homeless mentally ill individuals who cannot or will not access the social service system is the focus and challenge of outreach (Axelroad & Toff, 1987). Outreach encourages these persons to take advantage of available services and assists them with accessing these resources (Waxman, 1991). It is a dynamic approach that is performed in the client's own setting (Rog, Andranovich, & Rosenblum, 1987).

Outreach services may be mobile or stationary, depending on the needs of the target group. Outreach takes place in the streets, shelters, drop-in centers, medical emergency rooms, psychiatric emergency rooms, clients' homes, hospitals, and jails. Outreach programs also vary according to cultural settings and geographical areas (Axelroad & Toff, 1987). Active outreach is a critical step in fostering a sense of well-being, creating higher functioning, and encouraging independent living for homeless individuals. In order to accomplish its goals, the outreach method of service must be flexible, accessible, and non-threatening to clients.

Older adults are among the homeless mentally ill population receiving outreach. Older individuals of the general homeless population are also candidates for outreach because of poor physical health, physical frailty, and maladjustment to society's rapid pace (Heim, 1990). In addition, older persons who are at risk for homelessness can benefit from the outreach approach. Many older persons are vulnerable to displacement from their homes because of inadequate income, poor physical health, poor mental health, and lack of familial support. This is a serious situation, because without adequate mental health or medical treatment or necessary social services, their ability to remain in their residences is frequently in jeopardy (Heim, 1990). They need support and encouragement to maintain their current lifestyles. Many older individuals need assistance in escaping unstable and transient living arrangements as well.

Multidisciplinary teams are widely used in major cities throughout the United States to provide outreach to the homeless. Disciplines represented often include social work, mental health counseling, and nursing. Former homeless individuals are trained as outreach counselors. The choice of using one outreach worker or an entire team for individual clients varies among agencies. A holistic view is often used in outreach whereby one worker presents a blend of all disciplines. This is beneficial since it is necessary to be sensitive to the complexity of problems facing each homeless individual. The holistic approach blends mental health diagnosis, informal physical health examination, awareness of available social services and how a client can access them, as well as the ability to understand the steps to gain entitlements. Flexibilty in meeting the particular needs of each person is part of the holistic focus.

Due to the fragility of the client population encountered in outreach, there is an emphasis placed on continuity of care and trust between the outreach counselor and the individual (Axelroad & Toff, 1987). The target group consists of the most vulnerable and fragile street people. These persons are the most disabled of the homeless world and often are isolated from the service system and social networks. Additionally, they suffer from a lack of typical human interaction taken for granted by more fortunate individuals.

OUTREACH APPROACH

The first step in outreach is entering the community to locate and identify persons who need assistance. Observation of people on the streets, in shelters, or at soup kitchens must be made to determine those who are most vulnerable. Frequently, referrals are made from third parties (e.g., law enforcement, city employees, or local citizens). Hotel managers and landlords also may report problem residents who may be in danger of losing their home to a life in the streets.

From the outset, the outreach counselor needs to have an awareness of the neighborhood in which the target group members live. By examining and investigating the surroundings, these workers will better be able to understand the challenges facing specific clients. Heim (1990) suggests that to develop empathy a counselor should consider the following questions prior to contact with the client.

1. Are food stores and inexpensive eating areas nearby?
2. Are there senior and/or homeless meal programs nearby?
3. How busy is the street?
4. Is it safe for older or disabled persons to cross?

5. Is there drug traffic/prostitution nearby and, if so, how does this impact the neighborhood?
6. Is there a park nearby? If so, who frequents it?
7. Do any of the street people appear intimidating?
8. Are there nearby thrift shops?
9. Are there nearby labor pools?

Once the outreach counselor has evaluated the client's neighborhood, it is time to attempt to establish a relationship with the person. The outreach relationship is an interactive, two-way process between the homeless client and the counselor (Axelroad & Toff, 1987). In order to establish an interaction, efforts must be made to develop trust and rapport with the client. Respect for the autonomy of the homeless person is imperative. It is also important that the counselor honor the client's freedom to refuse participation at any stage in the relationship.

In maintaining a genuine, respectful attitude toward the homeless, the counselor must have an awareness of the conditions facing those living on the street as well as a knowledge of the ramifications of such conditions. A summary from the *Handbook for Outreach Volunteers* of Metropolitan Ministries of Tampa, Florida, indicates the following issues specified below:

1. *Continuous guarding for safety*: The homeless sleep lightly, infrequently, and poorly. Poor mental and physical health conditions are exacerbated by lack of sleep. The need to be on guard leads to suspicious, fearful behavior.
2. *Social isolation*: No eye contact, no acknowledgment from other people, and being ignored and avoided contribute to a sense of being invisible.
3. *Use of drugs or alcohol*: Frequently, those individuals who drink heavily do so because they find solace in the temporary relief from loneliness or frustration that alcohol provides. Sharing drinks and/or drugs is used by many to establish a sense of comradery with others.
4. *Poor diet*: Inadequate nutrition may contribute to biochemical imbalances. This may also exacerbate existing mental and physical health problems.

Unstable living conditions with constant disruptions and no opportunity to create routines or familiarity of surroundings contribute to the discouragement and frustration of a client. To cope with these difficult and dangerous conditions, homeless individuals frequently make unusual adjustments which appear unrealistic to those outside this environment. Workers need to realize that these adjustments are made within the world of reality as seen by the homeless, rather than the world as the counselor perceives it (Blankertz, Cnaan, White, Fox, & Messinger, 1990). Homeless people often struggle desperately to persevere and remain independent.

This struggle to remain independent and the insistence on that right often prevent clients from accepting assistance offered in a conventional manner. They may cling to their pride in having made it on the streets as their only source of self-esteem. Understanding this concept provides insight into the homeless person's situation and the struggle and need for autonomy. Unfortunately, the homeless frequently maintain a sense of dignity and self-determination that borders on self-destruction. In order to break this cycle, the outreach worker must meet these individuals on their own terms and within the framework of their numerous problems (Blankertz et al., 1990).

ESTABLISHING RELATIONSHIPS

In some instances, the strong need for autonomy and independence is countered by a strong need to be nurtured. When evident, this need should be encouraged by the outreach worker.

Paying the client unconditional respect is the first step in pursuing the relationship. This respect needs to be demonstrated beginning with the introduction. How the outreach counselor conducts this initial introduction is paramount to the success of the interaction and will determine the continuation of dialogue (Heim, 1990). Introducing oneself in a formal and respectful manner is best. The worker should identify himself or herself by name and give the name of the agency represented. Provision of a business card is not only a token of respect but enhances the possibility of continued communication. Workers must ask permission of clients to converse with them and enter their space (Blankertz et al., 1990). A counselor must be cognizant of the fact that most homeless are territorial of the area which they inhabit, regardless of whether it is a grate, box, or street block. This is a human trait not to be dismissed lightly. The length, rate, and choice of conversation is best left to the client. Once conversation is established, the counselor must not be abrupt when terminating the interaction (Blankertz et al., 1990).

To keep the homeless client from feeling threatened, it is necessary for the worker to allow a period of time for both the client and the counselor to adjust to the relationship and to feel comfortable with what each wishes to gain from the interaction (Blankertz et al., 1990). Empathetic listening is vital. Once rapport and trust have developed, the homeless client is often likely to perceive the outreach worker as the specific link to social services (Blankertz et al., 1990). The worker must be aware of this and also realize that the client will frequently test this perception to evaluate the seriousness and commitment of the counselor. The counselor needs to be prepared for this event.

It is helpful if the worker has good social skills. The outreach worker should act and talk in a normal manner, providing a model the client may emulate. This helps strengthen the self-esteem of clients as they discover a respectful, nonpatronizing, nonscornful relationship with another. Outreach workers also need to be aware of the necessity of providing a positive role model to clients. Homeless individuals frequently receive negative cues from those with whom they interact (Blankertz et al., 1990). As a result, after repeated occurrences, the homeless persons may adjust their behavior and expectations negatively. By giving positive messages to the client, the worker allows clients to change their outlook and motivates movement toward beneficial change.

At the onset of outreach, the worker must address the client's basic needs. This may be as simple as the offer of a sandwich and a blanket. Clients often find early discussion of mental or medical treatment intimidating, leading to distrust of the worker. It is best to begin with offers to assist in the procurement of food, clothing, and entitlements.

Counselors must be aware of verbal and nonverbal cues, theirs and the client's. By carrying an official-looking briefcase, the worker could unintentionally alienate a client by appearing with an item that is negatively construed as a symbol of bureaucracy (Blankertz et al., 1990). Counselors should know that each interaction and relationship will progress at its own rate. Progress is often slow. Being an outreach worker requires patience and perseverance. It needs to be recognized that progress in outreach is measured in "small, incremental gains" (Blankertz et al., 1990, p. 394).

Outreach services and staff need to be linked with community resources, including law enforcement, shelters, hospitals, sources of permanent housing, and rehabilitation programs, in order to know what services are available for the homeless client. A client needs to be well informed of what is anticipated and expected from the social service system should the choice be made to take advantage of assistance offered.

Homeless people lead lives characterized by frustration, anger, and disappointment; there must, therefore, be consistency between what is promised and what is provided. The outreach worker should be cautious when discussing services available. The worker must be honest regarding difficulties or delays that a client may encounter. Specificity in providing details is necessary so that the client is aware of what can and cannot be done. False promises lead to disappointment and distrust.

OUTREACH AND OLDER HOMELESS ADULTS

In working with disabled older homeless persons, the worker must be aware of the possibility of certain behaviors. Often during conversations, older adults may display long silences and demonstrate confusion (Heim,

1990). They may suffer hearing or vision loss, which contribute to poor communication. Workers should understand that older adults may perceive seeking mental health counseling as a weakness. This may exacerbate the reluctance of older homeless individuals to obtain assistance (Cohen & Sullivan, 1990). Older homeless people are vulnerable because of the lack of a "social margin at a time of life at which most people can expect to draw on that set of resources and relationships" (Doolin, 1986, p. 229). Resources might include pension plans, paid-in-full house mortgages, and the close relationship of a family.

Physical disorders are compounded by the stresses of homelessness. Because of life on the streets, older adults are found to age prematurely. Counselors should realize that an individual may be physiologically similar to those twenty years older yet chronologically ineligible for certain entitlements (Doolin, 1986).

In seeking social service programs for older homeless adults, workers must be aware that traditional senior service programs within the community may not be appropriate for the older homeless adult. Many of these programs tend to be ameliorative in nature. Upon initial entry into the service system, the needs of the older homeless may best be met in a rehabilitative program. It is often difficult to integrate the street adult into the social atmosphere created within services dominated by older housed adults (Doolin, 1986); however, options should remain open to assist the older homeless individual. The flexible, individually based approach of outreach counseling works best.

INTERVENTION

Once a relationship with a client has been established, the worker begins intervention. When working with the mentally ill population, the first step is to obtain a psychiatric or psychological assessment of the client to determine the mental health treatment that is needed for stabilization. Typically, care of the homeless mentally ill is provided by community mental health agencies funded by the McKinney Act.

Help is offered in a variety of approaches by outreach workers for homeless clients and those at risk for homelessness: obtaining medical treatment, assisting individuals in applying for entitlements, and placing the individual in educational and training programs (e.g., vocational rehabilitation or General Equivalency Diploma classes). When available, provision of housing is made. Frequently, workers assist clients in daily living tasks, such as management of budget and comparison shopping for groceries.

In total, services that may be provided in an outreach program for the homeless include food, clothing, shower facilities, transportation, residential services, health education, health screening and immunizations, medical services, mental health evaluations and services, assistance with benefits and entitlements, advocacy, guardianship status, and educational and training programs. Outreach workers are seen by Axelroad and Toff (1987) as viewing their major service to be that of ongoing case management.

Older homeless adults may have difficulty completing the necessary steps to access the various systems. An outreach worker may need to read print that is too small or help the person fill out lengthy applications for entitlements. Counselors often help older clients by scheduling appointments. The stressful lifestyle on the streets leaves many older homeless confused and forgetful. The worker can assist by reminding the client of appointments, providing bus vouchers, and plotting a bus route.

EMPOWERMENT

The most important assistance that the worker can offer the client is self-empowerment. Empowerment is the process that permits an individual to achieve that which is desired. By becoming empowered, a person develops the ability to accomplish goals. Developing and encouraging efforts that empower homeless individuals to attain the goals of reentry into society and development of autonomy is of vital importance.

Addressing basic needs of the homeless population has been attempted in communities across the nation. Improvement and expansion of resources and the creation of additional new services is ongoing. Policy makers are planning long-term solutions, such as creation of low-income housing or a national health plan, that will help relieve the despair. To further advance solutions to homelessness, increased emphasis must be placed on undertakings that enable the homeless to help themselves.

Empowerment of the homeless to accomplish reintegration and independence may be enhanced by implementation of various strategies. We include a few suggestions. When these suggestions are put to use, the outcome of increased self-worth often results. Creating an atmosphere in which the homeless individual can fulfill the basic human need to feel accepted, safe, secure, and of value and benefit to society provides a springboard to meet positive goals.

EMPOWERMENT STRATEGIES

Aristotle stated that "all must vote or none can remain free." Janice Grady, a former homeless person who is now on the staff of the National Coalition for the Homeless, spoke out regarding her experience with voting rights during her period of homelessness. She stated, "to some, this [voting rights] might appear to be a small issue. But to me, it meant being recognized as someone who matters" (*National Coalition for the Homeless*, 1992, p. 1).

Utilizing the right to vote empowers the homeless individual in various ways. As illustrated by Grady's statement, acknowledging one's right as a citizen to vote as part of the democratic process of this country promotes a sense of self-worth and self-respect. The act of registering to vote aids the homeless individual in obtaining a form of identification. Because most agencies assisting the homeless require formal proof of identification, a voter registration card may furnish the first step for an individual to acquire benefits and services. Such services may afford the stabilization necessary to reenter society.

Voter registration drives, when aimed specifically at the homeless, demonstrate to communities that persons without a home have the right, as well as the interest, to protect their civil liberties and to shape public policy. This awareness helps to dispel the stereotypical attitude often held in society that all homeless persons are shiftless transient hobos. It makes the general public more aware that the homeless are indeed citizens with all the rights of citizenship. With increasing numbers voting as a block, persons without a home can have more and more influence on elected public officials. They gain political voice, thus being able to take positive strides toward having their problems addressed (Coates, 1990).

Filing income tax returns is part of empowerment. Paul Heimer, Volunteer Coordinator of the Salvation Army of the Alexandria Community Shelter in Alexandria, Virginia (personal communication, July, 1992), provided the following information on how to assist homeless individuals with preparation of income tax returns. Volunteer Income Tax Assistance (VITA) is a division of the Internal Revenue Service and will train agency or volunteer staff involved in homeless issues on tax laws so that they can aid homeless persons in filing a return. Training sessions are usually held in December. Contact the local IRS VITA representative for assistance. Heimer suggests that the trained workers assist the homeless clients individually in the process of filing. "Teaching people how to file will ensure that they continue to file," states Mr. Heimer (personal communication, July, 1992).

The volunteer guides the taxpayer through the appropriate form line by line. Asking the person to read a few lines will quickly allow the volunteer to determine if the client is literate. The homeless client needs to receive sufficient instruction in order to continue the practice of filing a return in subsequent years. Stressing self-help is the key to empowerment. It is suggested that agencies involve college students majoring in accounting or other related fields to act as volunteers. Involvement of the media is encouraged so that interested parties are made aware of the availability of the self-help program and community interest is aroused. Filing an income tax return empowers a homeless individual in a manner similar to voting; it gives a person a sense of achievement for conquering what may appear to be an insurmountable task. A tax refund can be used as a rent or utility deposit or for other constructive use.

Education equips one with a sense of competence. Development of skills and aptitudes provides not only the tools a person needs to enter the wage-earning world but develops self-worth and confidence as well. The following areas may be of assistance in empowering the homeless: literacy classes, vocational rehabilitation, adult education courses, GED preparation, technical schools, and community colleges/universities.

Transitional housing offers stable shelter for an extended period of time. It provides and environment between that of a shelter and rental or ownership of one's own residence. This pasage of time offers the homeless individual the structure and support to learn how to be self-reliant. A small rental fee is generally required, as is payment for groceries. Contributing to one's keep gives one a sense of involvement and pride.

Chores that may appear routine to mainstream society can promote a sense of accomplishment in those who have not recently experienced daily living tasks. The lengthy and continuous stay in transitional housing when conducted within hospitable surroundings encourages the development of a social support system. When family and friends are available in the outside community, these bonds are given the chance to be strengthened as well. Developing a network of friends contributes to a sense of worth and stability (Russell, 1991).

Dental services are greatly needed by homeless individuals in our society. Funding for community resources is scarce and must be distributed for many needs. Unfortunately, provision of dental care is not often given high priority. Repairing teeth benefits one physically and is essential for maintaining a nutritious diet. In addition to contributing to good health, filling gaps (with a partial plate, dentures, or a bridge) that have blemished an individual's appearance proves to be extremely beneficial in boosting self-esteem. Those who have poor dental hygiene and missing teeth are shunned by our society and are seen as unlikely candidates for most employment. The remedies of dentistry can empower the homeless individual who seeks to acquire meaningful work placement.

CONCLUSION

A report to the National Institute of Mental Health, Office of Programs for the Homeless Mentally Ill on the McKinney Mental Health Services for the Homeless Block Grant Program (Adler, 1991) indicates that most programs stress outreach and intensive case management as the key services needed for the homeless mentally ill. *Access*, a publication of the National

Resource Center on Homelessness and Mental Illness, reports that access to existing programs and improving outreach efforts is one of the four primary goals around which the Federal Task Force on Homelessness and Severe Mental Illness has organized its national action plan (National Resource Center, 1992). The Task Force report (Health and Human Services, 1992) asserts that attempts to help homeless people with severe mental illnesses must address all aspects of their life situation. Outreach is often a lengthy and frustrating process, requiring patience and flexibility from counselors. There are many obstacles in serving the entire homeless population, but they are not insurmountable.

REFERENCES

Adler, W. C. (1991). *Addressing homelessness: Status of programs under the Stewart B. McKinney Assistance Act and related legislation.* Washington, DC: National Governors' Association.

Axelroad, S. E., & Toff, G. E. (1987). *Outreach services for homeless mentally ill people.* Washington, DC: Intergovernmental Health Policy Project.

Blankertz, L. E., Cnaan, R. A., White, K., Fox, J., & Messinger, K. (1990). Outreach efforts with dually diagnosed homeless persons. *Families in Society: The Journal of Contemporary Human Services, 71,* 387-397.

Coates, R. (1990). *A street is not a home.* Buffalo, NY: Prometheus Books.

Cohen, N. L., & Sullivan, A. M. (1990). Strategies of intervention and service coordination by mobile outreach teams. In N. L. Cohen (Ed.), *Psychiatry takes to the streets* (pp. 63-79). New York: Guilford Press.

Doolin, J. (1986). Planning for the special needs of the homeless elderly. *The Gerontologist, 26,* 229-231.

Handbook for outreach volunteers. Unpublished data. Tampa, FL: Metropolitan Ministries, Inc.

Health and Human Services. (1992, February). *Outcasts on Main Street: Report of the Federal Task Force on Homelessness.* Washington, DC: Health and Human Services.

Heim, P. (1990). Psychiatric outreach to the elderly in downtown San Francisco. In N. L. Cohen (Ed.), *Psychiatry takes to the streets* (pp. 210-228). New York: Guilford Press.

National Coalition for the Homeless. (1992). *Safety Network, II,* 1-4.

National Resource Center on Homelessness and Mental Illness. (1992). *Access, 4,* 1-4. Washington, DC: National Resource Center on Homelessness and Mental Illness.

Rog, D. J., Andranovich, G. D., & Rosenblum, S. (1987). *Intensive case management for persons who are homeless and mentally ill* (Vol. 1, Contract 278-86-0014, Institute of Mental Health). Washington, DC: Cosmos Corporation.

Russell, B. (1991). *Silent sisters.* New York: Hemisphere Publishing Corporation.

Waxman, L. D. (1991). *A status report on hunger and homelessness in America's cities: 1991.* Washington, DC: The United States Conference of Mayors.

ARA
services

11

Community Resources

Judith Sullivan-Mintz

Resources in communities across the United States have been created, expanded, or adjusted to meet the needs of homeless individuals. Although attempts are being made by programs nationwide, numerous gaps remain. Endeavors are hampered by reluctance and the difficulty many homeless have in accessing resources. Cuts in social spending have compounded problems facing community programs; additionally, poor economic times increase demands. Positive steps are being made to aid homeless individuals to return to a productive life. Examples of innovative programming follow.

COMMUNITY EFFORTS IN THE NATION

1. *The Kit Clark Senior Center* in Boston, Massachusetts makes available adult day shelter, transportation, and restaurant-style meals for Boston's older homeless (Doolin, 1986).
2. *The Home Medical Service*, connected with the Boston Housing Authority, provides temporary shelter for older homeless persons. Six rent-free units are set aside as temporary shelter exclusively for older homeless adults. Those eligible may stay for up to forty-five days and are allowed three 15-day extensions (Coates, 1990).
3. The *state lottery* proceeds in Pennsylvania are used for older citizen programs. Free public transportation is provided for older adults (Coates, 1990). This is extremely beneficial to homeless individuals, as lack of transportation is often the missing link in obtaining vital services.

The following programs, though not specifically targeted for older homeless adults, illustrate how progressive communities across the country are approaching the problems of homelessness.

1. *Burnside Projects* in Portland, Oregon provides a 114-bed shelter with many services. These include alcohol treatment, an employment program, alcohol-free housing, mental health treatment, correctional services, pretrial supervision, money management, food and Single Residency Occupancy hotels (SROs) (Fike, 1990).
2. Baloney Joe's (Portland, Oregon) operates in a renovated warehouse where food is available through a non-profit cafe. Other resources are clothing, laundry, medical and dental services (Fike, 1990).
3. *The Downtown Service Center* in Nashville, Tennessee provides day shelter to over 200 homeless persons per day and offers alcohol and drug counseling, showers, laundry, medical and dental treatment, information and referral. A food stamp worker is on site to assist (Waxman, 1991).
4. *Unity Inn, House of Ruth* is transitional housing for women in Washington, DC. This half-way house emphasizes mutual support among the women and independent living skills (Fike, 1990).
5. The *Homeward Literacy Initiative grant* awarded to the Adult Basic Education Department, Hillsborough County School Board, Florida (J. Perez, personal communication, April 7, 1992) provides a reading program for homeless individuals who read at a low level, or not at all. Adult Basic Education works cooperatively with the Hillsborough County Coalition for the Homeless to provide agency space for classes and implements the outreach portion of the program.
6. *Share Tampa Bay* is a program of United Methodist Centers, Tampa, Florida. This self-supporting operation, funded by participants, provides food packages. Each participant exchanges a small payment, cash or food stamps, and monthly volunteer service for a food package valued at twice the stipend paid. Payment covers cost of food and operation of the program with the volunteer hours providing labor (Hillsborough County Coalition for the Homeless, 1994).

LOCAL COALITIONS FOR THE HOMELESS

Homeless individuals living in the Tampa Bay area are provided services that include shelter, food, clothing, on-site meals, showers, day centers, outreach programs, medical care, mental health care, alcohol and drug rehabilitation, emergency dental treatment, literacy programs, job training, transportation, programs for ex-offenders, and housing.

Hillsborough and Pinellas Counties each have formed coalitions for the homeless. Hillsborough County established the Hillsborough County Coalition for the Homeless in 1986 in response to the Statewide Task Force on the Homeless with goals to "coordinate services, interchange information, evaluate homeless services, advocate for the homeless, increase community awareness, and plan future service directions" (Hillsborough County Board of Commissioners, 1990, p. 2). Among coalition members are representatives of private shelters, law enforcement, church groups, mental health providers, alcohol and drug agencies, and others. The Hillsborough County Coalition for the Homeless is an expanding organization with over 100 members and the Pinellas County Coalition for the Homeless is similar in structure. It is seen as the "cornerstone of the coordinated community planning effort . . . attempting to effectively and efficiently meet the needs of a growing homeless population" (Pinellas, 1990, p. 1). The two coalitions are beginning a cooperative effort to share information about effective programs in each county. Each coalition publishes a resource guide for the homeless.

CASE STUDIES USING COMMUNITY RESOURCES

Composite case studies of homeless persons in Tampa Bay illustrate utilization of community resources.

Case #1 - Vincent is a 52-year-old African American male who arrives in Tampa from Ohio. On the night of his arrival, he is beaten and robbed. He has neither clothes, money, job, identification, nor a social or economic support system. He does not wish to return to Ohio. He says, "There's nothing there for me either."

Immediate goal: Survival needs
Long range goal: Employment to maintain these needs

Possible Community Resources

Food: Metropolitan Ministries (multipurpose center for the homeless), soupline, breakfast, lunch

Salvation Army, dinner

Clothes: Metropolitan Ministries Outreach Department

Injury: Sine Domus Walk-In Clinic for the Homeless

Identification: Metropolitan Ministry Outreach Department may issue client referral letter for Office of the Social Security Administration to reapply for lost/stolen Social Security card.

Employment: Labor pools (two companies have pick-up at Metropolitan Ministries). Register for Florida Job Service.

Identification: Refer to HRS Vital Statistics Bureau for birth certificate. Once obtained, refer client to State of Florida License Bureau to obtain picture ID.

Shelter: Two free nights at the Salvation Army.

Food Stamps: Once he has ID and is registered for work, he is eligible to apply for food assistance. He can obtain a letter from Metropolitan Ministries informing the HRS Food Stamp Program that he is homeless without a place of residence.

Case #2 - Henry is a 65-year-old white male, and a veteran of World War II. He refuses to go to a nursing home and prefers living on street. He applied for Social Security benefits but has not been receiving his checks because he has no address. He suffers from phlebitis, which is exacerbated by continuous walking and standing. He experiences a constant cough and is afraid he may have tuberculosis. He doesn't want to go into a nursing home but is afraid he will die if he stays on the streets.

Immediate Goal: Health concerns

Long Range Goal: Acceptable living arrangement

Possible Community Resources

Outreach: Contact Veterans Center Outreach Program at Metropolitan Ministries.

Benefits: Homeless persons are permitted to use Metropolitan Ministries address for mail. The VA counselor may inform the Social Security Administration of Henry's new address.

Health: VA counselor may arrange for physical exam at James A. Haley Veterans Hospital.

Day care: While Henry waits for benefits, exam, etc., VA refers him to ACTS Day Center so that he may have a place to rest during the day.

Transitional: VA counselor may arrange entry into Bay Pines Domiciliary, temporary living facility for homeless veterans. Shelter, food, medical, counseling, search for housing provided. Opportunity for individual to stabilize.

Permanent: Placement on waiting list with the St. Petersburg Housing Authority for low-rent housing units for older people.

Case #3 - Sue-Ann is a white, well-dressed female, age 56. She is divorced with no children. She suffered a recent catastrophic illness and still requires medical attention. She has depleted resources and social ties. She has been living in a shelter for the last two weeks, but she moved out because she said it was "uncomfortable" and "unsafe." She appears paranoid and depressed. Her physical appearance indicates poor health.

Immediate Goal: Evaluate physical and mental health

Long Term Goal: Stabilization of client regarding both physical and mental health

Possible Community Resources

Outreach: Sine Domus Walk-In Clinic for the Homeless

Referral: Sine Domus may refer client to County Hospital for treatment of illness. Travel arrangements provided by bus vouchers or Share-A-Van.

Referral: Sine Domus might recommend psychiatric services and short term case management could be provided by Baylife Network Project.

Case #4 - Manny is a 38-year-old Puerto Rican male alcohol and drug addict. He was just released from prison for possession of cocaine. Frightened and lonely on the streets, he is desperately afraid he will resume drinking and taking drugs. He has no job and no place to live. He would like to return to his family in Puerto Rico, but he does not have the means to do so.

Short Term Goal: Meet basic needs

Long Term Goal: Alcohol/drug addiction recovery

Possible Community Resources

Food: Metropolitan Ministries, Salvation Army

Shelter: Choices available: Salvation Army, Abundant Life, Lighthouse Gospel Mission

Outreach: Referral to be made by Sine Domus for client to enter residential alcohol and drug treatment program where space is available: Alcohol Community Treatment Service; Metropolitan Ministries Manna House

Support: Establish relationship with ACTION, INC., a program to help ex-offenders with outreach counseling, motivation, and referral service, or Prison Crusade, a group that provides spiritual guidance, job guidance and counseling for ex-offenders

IMPROVEMENTS IN COMMUNITY RESOURCES

The community resource system is necessary for survival. Dear and Wolch (1987) point out how entangled causes and solutions of homeless problems are. The system of numerous agencies, services, centers, and shelters is caring but is stretched beyond its limits. With waiting lists and lines, restrictive eligibility criteria, and bureaucratic intrusion, the homeless person often becomes discouraged, depressed, and eventually dependent on the very system that wishes to create independence. As resources for homelessness programs improve, community programs must improve access and availability of services so the procedures are less demeaning. Current HUD programs wisely emphasize the need for a continuum of care with three components: emergency shelter, transitional housing with social services, and permanent housing (U. S. Department of Housing and Urban Development, 1994).

Fike (1990) suggests improvements to the community resource system, such as: (1) early outreach for the newly homeless prior to adaptation; (2) service provision in various areas of cities, rather than centralized in downtown; and (3) recognition and treatment of depression.

Older homeless adults would benefit from such ideas. Advocates for older individuals must encourage specialized programs and services for homeless persons age 50+ who may be mentally and physically handicapped and need extra support to survive. Homeless older adults have the fewest social supports and are the most disenfranchised group in our country, surviving on public assistance of the lowest level (Doolin, 1986).

INNOVATIVE APPROACHES

1. *The National Endowment for the Arts* made a grant to the city of Boston for a design competition focusing on the need for safe and affordable housing for people with AIDS. The city and the Boston Society of Architects cosponsored the competition.

2. *The Artists' Collective* helps homeless artists sell their work through mail order, on consignment, and at neighborhood table sales. Contact Voices and Visions from the Margins, South Press, 343 Broadway, Dobbs Ferry, NY 10522.
3. *Greetings for Food* employs homeless artists to design greeting cards for retail sale. Artists are paid royalties for their work. Contact Greetings for Food, Inc., Peter B. Ashley, Executive Director, P.O. Box 40048, Philadelphia, PA 19106.
4. *Rodale Press of Manhattan* sponsors an organic garden on the rooftop of a homeless shelter. The firm donates soil, seeds, etc., and residents of the shelter tend the garden. The garden provides fresh vegetables for the shelter, and workers gain job experience. Contact Grand Central Partnership, 6 East 43rd Street, Suite 2100, New York, NY 10017.
5. *Hellger Communications*, a phone service firm in Indianapolis, helps the homeless find employment by providing free private number voice mail at four local shelters and missions.
6. *McMurphy's Grill* in St. Louis, Missouri offers job training to homeless mentally ill people. The restaurant runs a skills workshop on budgeting, parenting, tenant responsibility, and personal hygiene, 12 sessions in all. Contact St. Patrick Center, D. Henroid, Executive Director, 1200 N. 6th Street, St. Louis, MO 63106. Phone (314)621-1283.
7. *Work-a-Thon* is sponsored by the National Student Campaign Against Hunger and Homelessness. Volunteer participants raise money by signing up sponsors to pledge money for hours that participants work in community agencies.
8. *The Job Fair* of the Junior League of Northern Virginia focuses on special employment needs of homeless persons. Prior to the fair, seminars are held for resume writing, job interview practice, etc. Local employees are recruited to offer positions, and the Junior League provides transportation and baby sitting.
9. *Centerplace for the Homeless* offers services such as employment counseling for older workers and an adult education teacher to help client prepare for the GED. Contact Suzanne Krebsbach, Centerplace for Homeless,

1924 Taylor Street, Columbia, SC 29201. Phone (803)254-2103.

10. *The Federal Surplus Property Program*, created under the Stewart B. McKinney Homeless Assistance Act, requires that certain unused federally owned properties be made available to agencies helping the homeless. The Mental Health and Mental Retardation Services in San Angelo, Texas acquired property used for independent living facilities for up to seven of the program participants. Contact James Young, Executive Director, MHMR Services for Concho Valley, 1501 W. Beauregard, San Angelo, TX 76901. Phone (915)658-7750.
11. *Shelter Partnership*, a not-for-profit organization in a contract with the Los Angeles, California Housing Authority, received an Award of Merit from the National Association of Housing and Redevelopment in the category of program innovation for assisting homeless families and disabled individuals in obtaining permanent housing. Contact Shelter Partnership, 1010 South Flower Street, Suite 400, Los Angeles, CA 90015.
12. *Step Up on 2nd* offers outreach and follow-up services to help formerly homeless mentally ill adults who have moved into affordable, independent or group living situations. Contact Susan Dempsey, 1328 Second Street, Santa Monica, CA. Phone (310)395-8886.
13. *Compadre* is a training course designed for volunteers and social service staff to "foster economic and psychological self-sufficiency for very low-income families and the elderly wishing to remain independent." A team approach focuses on restoring independent living for the client. Contact San Antonio Housing Authority Foundation, Inc., Dennis Duggin, Program Director, P.O. Box 1300, San Antonio, TX 78295.
14. *Volunteer Income Tax Assistance* trains homeless agency volunteers and staff to assist individuals with income tax forms. Contact Internal Revenue Service at 1-800-829-1040. Registration for VITA training takes place in January of each year. Local sites are often available.
15. *The Homeward Literacy Initiative Grant* helps homeless individuals with poor or no reading skills. Contact Joe Perez, Supervisor, Hillsborough County Schools, 4602 N. Seminole, Tampa, FL 33603.
16. *Shelter-Pak* is a coat that serves as a sleeping bag and folds into a 2-pound bag. It can be made on home sewing

machines using lightweight fabric. Volunteers are involved in assembly. Contact Philadelphia College of Textiles and Science, Jean McAulay, Director of Public Relations, School House Lane and Henry Lane, Philadelphia, PA 19144-5497. Phone (212)951-2851.

17. *The Homeless Support Initiative Program* provides blankets. Applications are accepted at any time on a continuing basis. Contact Bill Gala, Defense Logistic Agency, Headquarters Cameron Station, Attn: DLA-ORM, Alexandria, VA 22304-6100. Phone (703)274-6361.
18. *Pioneer Human Services*, a Seattle nonprofit organization, operates as a business enterprise rather than as a typical charitable agency. Housing, job training/employment, education, case management, and health-care benefits are provided. Contact HUD USER, P.O. Box 6091, Rockville, MD 20850. Phone 1-800-245-2691.
19. *Project Rescue* (Cohen et al., 1992) is a coed program for older homeless individuals in the Bowery of New York City. This is a day program restricted to those age 60+. Project Rescue is a multi-service agency that attempts to meet the needs of older homeless and marginally homeless persons. The agency provides a respite program, breakfast, and lunch. Other services include assistance with housing, financial and vocational application, and social programs. A medical team and psychiatric and alcohol service components are also available.
20. *Representative payees* assist homeless people in managing benefits, receiving checks on behalf of the beneficiary, and providing for their personal needs. Contact Louise Ross, Office of Public Affairs, Social Security Administration, P.O. Box 17743, Baltimore, MD 21235. Phone (410)965-4031.
21. *Clean and Sober* is an alcohol/drug treatment program in 13 homeless shelters in Philadelphia that provides a therapeutic community where program participants assume responsibility for development and recovery. Contact Leslie Brown, 401 North Broad Street, Suite 230, Philadelphia, PA 19108. Phone (215)477-1918.
22. *Housing Initiatives for Homeless People with Alcohol/Drug Problems* documents the conference cosponsored by the National Institute on Alcohol Abuse and Alcoholism. Contact National Clearinghouse for Alcohol and Drug

Information, P.O. Box 2345, Rockville, MD 20852. Phone 1-800-729-6686.

CONCLUSION

Political, social, and economic assistance must be in place to enhance resources within the community so that all homeless citizens may live in dignity. A movement must address the dilemma of discouragement and defeat voiced by an older homeless alcoholic, quoted by Doolin (1986, p. 230): "An old bum ain't nothin' but an old bum."

REFERENCES

Coates, R. C. (1990). *A street is not a home.* Buffalo, NY: Prometheus Books.

Cohen, C. I., Onsevud, H. & Monaco, C., (1992) Project Rescue: Serving the homeless and marginally housed elderly. *The Gerontologist*, *32*(4), 466-471.

Dear, M. J., & Wolch, J. R. (1987). *Landscapes of despair.* Princeton, NJ: Princeton University Press.

Doolin, J. (1986). Planning for the special needs of the homeless elderly. *The Gerontologist*, *26*, 229-231.

Fike, D. F. (1990). *The South Florida homelessness studies of 1989.* A summary of key findings (Vol. 4). Miami, FL: Barry University.

Hillsborough County Board of Commissioners, Department of Community Services and Planning. (1990). *Hillsborough County's comprehensive homeless assistance plan (CHAP)* (Publication No. 90-1311). Tampa, FL: Department of Community Services and Planning.

Hillsborough County Coalition for the Homeless. (1994). *Resource Guide.* Tampa, FL: Hillsborough County Coalition for the Homeless.

Pinellas County Homeless Coalition. (1990). *Winter 1990 homeless survey.* St. Petersburg, FL: Pinellas County Homeless Coalition.

U. S. Department of Housing and Urban Development Office of Community Planning and Development (1994, April). Continuum of care: A complete approach to meet the homeless needs. *Community Connections*, pp. 1, 3.

Waxman, L. D. (1991). *Mentally ill and homeless: A 22 city survey.* Washington, DC: The United States Conference of Mayors.

12

Housing Overview

Irena M. Zuk

Although we have all become more sensitive to the tragedy of homelessness, early media depictions of the stereotypical homeless person still encourage images of bag ladies and bums. Yet the term *homeless* merely reflects the phenomenon of being without a home.

According to Keigher and Pratt (1991), housing for older adults has deteriorated to such a great extent over the past decade that it has become a precipitating factor in homelessness. This deterioration has paralleled the erosion of publicly supported housing options for the older adult since the 1980s. With the shortage of low-rent housing, more older adults will continue to find themselves among the homeless. In 1991, Keigher and Pratt's research showed few plans for more construction in the future. Funds for assisted housing went from $25 billion in FY 1981 to $8.9 billion in FY 1990. Low-income renters in that timespan (1974-1988) increased by 56 percent (Burt, 1992), with older adults and families with children making up the greater proportion of this group. Burt (1992) reported that between 1980 and 1983, 6 million more people reached the poverty level. Forty-five percent of public housing (1.2 million units) was occupied by older adults, who had to contend with the dangers of dilapidated buildings and drug trafficking. Even these housing options were not available to them for long. During the Bush Administration, it was recommended that the units be sold to tenants or private investors (Keigher & Pratt, 1991).

Schwartz, Ferlauto, and Hoffman (1988) noted that 50 percent of those older adults who own their own homes live in poverty. According to Torres-Gil (1992), this percentage would be even higher if poverty levels for older adults were not artificially lowered by the government. The poverty level for those age 65+ is marked by an annual income of $5,447; for those under 65, it is $5,909. If the same criteria were used for both groups, older adults would make up the greatest percentage of those in poverty. However, notes Torres-Gil (1992), even under the lower standard, 4 million live in poverty and an additional 4.4 million live within 150 percent of the poverty index--most of these older adults are women and minorities.

HISTORY: FEDERAL HOUSING POLICIES

The Health Care for Homeless People Committee (Committee on Health Care, 1988) indicated that the government recognized its obligation to ensure decent housing for every American with the National Housing Act of 1938. The retreat from this commitment can be seen in the dramatic escalation of the numbers who are homeless. Those in need of housing, created partially by deinstitutionalizationduring the 1950s and 1960s, increased tremendously as a result of landlords of low-income housing who prepaid on HUD mortgages. Furthermore, according to Wiener (1990), the following seven developments in federal housing legislation contributed to the current housing shortage:

1. The Farmer's Home Administration (FmHA) subsidized rent of older adults with Section 515 of the Rural Rental Housing Program. Created by the Senior Citizens Act of 1962, this program provided long-term rental and cooperative housing for low-income older adults. The government offered direct subsidized loans to stimulate production of low-income housing.
2. Congressional stipulations were made that owners were required to prepay government loans as soon as they could obtain private loans at reasonable rates. Between 1972 and 1986, over 900 mortgages financed through FmHA Section 515 were being paid off and low-income units were converted to market rate housing.
3. FmHA 1972 restrictions on loans to limited-profit entities encouraged prepayment. Building owners received loans at very low interest rates and a 5 percent equity contribution, needing only to agree to lower rents. This guaranteed them rental payments and a shelter against depreci-ation. Once property appreciated and the tax shelter expired (7 to 10 years), they could take the option of prepayment.
4. Congress introduced legislation in 1979 forbidding prepayment of a full 50-year mortgage. It admitted to insufficient foresight in 1972.
5. One year later, with strenuous opposition from the building industry, the 1979 legislation was repealed and replaced with a 20-year restriction stipulation. Loans received pre-1980 could still be prepaid (200,000 units fell into the pre-1980 category). This was the beginning of the housing shortage problem that we

now face. Older adult and other low-income residents, faced with rents beyond their means, experienced severe financial, emotional, and physical hardship.

6. Congress passed the Housing Act of 1987, authorizing FmHA to offer owners incentives not to prepay and making prepayment more difficult. However, since May of 1988, owners of 200 projects (6,800 units) have made requests for prepayment. This Act handicapped the housing situation further by diverting total dollars from new construction.
7. In 1989, Congress eliminated the prepayment option in all prospective Section 515 projects. However, it did not address the more than 50 percent of inventory of units whose 20-year restrictions will expire in the year 2000. This federal housing legislation has greatly contributed to the lack of low-income housing and subsequent housing and homeless problems.

1992-1995 BUDGET PROPOSALS

The Clinton Administration has drafted the first federal plan to address homelessness as a chronic national problem (What, 1994). Under the Clinton Administration, there have been significant budget increases for Homeless Assistance Programs, as indicated in Table 12.1. President Clinton's 1995 budget proposal seeks more than $1.7 billion for HUD homeless assistance programs, twice the appropriation of the previous year. This budget proposal indicates that the Administration recognizes the tremendous scope of the problems (U. S. Department of Housing and Urban Development, 1994).

Table 12.1
Budget Increases for HUD Homeless Assistance Programs
Source: *Budget Authority for 1992, 1993, 1994 Enacted and 1995 President's Budget Request.*

Year	Budget
1992	$490 million
1993	$600 million
1994	$850 million
1995	$1.7 billion

PSYCHOSOCIAL MAKEUP OF OLDER HOMELESS ADULTS

Researchers (Keigher & Pratt, 1991) have ascertained that older homeless adults present a common psychosocial picture: They are poor; have lost low-income housing; are jobless; have little formal education; have limited employment potential; have little social support; have a history of tragedy and failure; and often have lessened mental capabilities resulting in inability to manage funds.

OLDER ADULTS AMONG THE HOMELESS POPULATION

Wright (1989) and Doolin (1985) report that it is the lack of low-cost rental units which has increased the visibility of the older adult among the homeless. Doolin agrees with Torres-Gil (1992) that 15 percent (4 million) older adults live in poverty. These authors, as well as Levin and Stockdill (1984), note that conversion of single units into condominiums and high-rent apartments presented an unexpected expense that older adults could not meet.

Single-resident occupancies (SROs) were good alternatives for low-income individuals, according to Keigher (1991). However, with the federal 1991 budget cut proposal, this housing became part of the Shelter Plus Care program, limited to the mentally ill and recovering substance abusers.

Between 1970 and 1980, 1 million SROs were eliminated (*The Harvard Mental Health Letter*, July, 1990). In New York City alone, available units went from 170,000 in 1971 to 14,000 in 1984. Ovrebo, Minkler, and Liljestrand (1991) believe that the nation's policy of deserving and undeserving poor has played a role in the disappearance of SROs. Although they are an extremely important alternate housing option, many of these buildings have been replaced with highrises to serve the needs of young urban professionals (the deserving) without regard for low-income tenants (the undeserving). The loss of SROs has contributed not only to the number of homeless older adults but also to the numbers who were institutionalized as a result. Older adults still in SROs are being pushed out by landlords who wish to renovate and expand for gentrification (Hudson, Rauch, Dawson, Santos, & Burdick, 1990). This leaves most older adults unable to relocate into areas where they can afford services or find equivalents of their former support networks (Hudson et al., 1990; Keigher & Pratt, 1991).

The vital importance of SROs is that they provide a social network (Keigher & Pratt, 1991) which establishes a beneficent psychological support system. SROs are a convenient and reasonably priced alternative for older adults. Unfortunately, rents have risen to such a degree that many older adults can no longer afford even this housing. Today's homeless have approximately one third the income of those in the 1950s (Rossi, 1990). In New York City, SRO residents spend an average of 73 percent of their income on rent (Ovrebo et al., 1991). Not only do older homeless adults lose shelter with the loss of SROs, but they also lose vital informal helping networks, which they do not otherwise readily find on their own (Hudson et al., 1990; Keigher, 1991).

Fortunately, many cities, aware that older adults could survive independently in SROs, are beginning to renovate them (Hudson et al., 1990) through funding from the McKinney Act of 1987, which allocated funds for such renovations as well as special funds for older homeless adults. Its success can only be judged by how these funds are administered for this purpose (Hudson et al., 1990).

Contributing further to the housing shortage is the rise of arson in these sub-standard housing areas (Doolin, 1985; Wright, 1989). This crime is spreading and leaving whole neighborhoods devastated (Doolin, 1985). Such developments are strategic factors in the series of events contributing to homelessness. According to Hudson et al. (1990), many older adults are left without friends and family supports and their survival skills diminish, leaving them more vulnerable on the streets. Keigher and Greenblatt (1992) report that support received from living with another person greatly reduces the risk of homelessness for the older adult. This living arrangement not only provides an emotional stronghold but also another income, better coping mechanisms for stress, and as a result, prevention of loss of home. Even shelters do not provide a haven for the older adult. They consider them dangerous and are squeezed out by younger homeless, who often abuse them verbally and physically (Committee on Health Care, 1988; Doolin, 1985).

DEINSTITUTIONALIZATION

The debate continues as to whether deinstitutionalization caused an increase in homelessness. Hudson et al. (1990) report general agreement that the great numbers of homeless mentally ill are a result of deinstitutionalization. This movement was planned poorly and did not allow for development and funding of programs to handle the needs of this new segment of society. Although deinstitutionalization certainly contributed to homelessness, Tessler and Dennis (1989) stress that it has not been the major cause of homelessness. The authors believe that this theory may have developed because many homeless have psychiatric problems, but this does not make homelessness a product of deinstitutionalization. Doolin (1986) agrees that, for the most part, older homeless adults are not a product of deinstitutionalization but are victims of higher living costs.

ECONOMIC FACTORS

The pressing need for subsidized housing can only be fully appreciated when we consider that between 1974 and 1987, the numbers of households with incomes of $5,000 and less grew from 2.7 million to 4.7 million (Keigher, Berman, & Greenblatt, 1991). Instead of an increase in housing projects, federally subsidized HUD housing decreased 80 percent from 167,000 units per year to 25,000 units. Another 1 million units became unavailable because of discontinued low-income restrictions.

Burt (1992) reports that after 1981, federal housing assistance no longer added new units to low-cost housing. This added further pressure on rent levels and reduced affordability for those with lower incomes (Burt, 1992). In addition to a lack of affordable housing, unemployment greatly added to the increased numbers of the homeless (Hudson et al., 1990). According to Burt (1992), there was an increase of 3.9 million poor people from 1970 to 1980 (15 percent), increasing the poverty rate from 12.6 percent to 13.0 percent and between 1980 and 1983, 6 million additional people reached the poverty level. Federal assistance is provided to those with low income via the Section 8 voucher program (Keigher, 1991). HUD assists with payment for the difference between a unit's actual rent and 30 percent adjusted tenant income. While providing more housing options for older adults, HUD unfortunately increases the likelihood that more than 30 percent of income goes toward rent, especially in higher cost urban areas (Keigher & Pratt, 1991).

Benefits are not always as helpful as they might appear to be on the Senate floor. One can only speculate if anyone was present in the Senate when the Bush Administration reduced housing construction for older adults and the handicapped by 53 percent (Keigher, 1991). The resulting housing shortage left an average of six Section 8 units available for every 1,000 older adults.

INNOVATIVE SOLUTIONS AND FEDERAL ASSISTANCE

O'Connell, Summerfield, and Kellogg (1990) report on the *Senior Reach Program*, a resettlement service for older adults in Chicago funded by the Chicago Department of Aging and Disability. Problem resolution takes an average of four months, although the process can take up to 12 months; this program is especially beneficial for older homeless adults distrustful of shelters and clinics.

Project Rescue (The Bowery, New York City) was developed to serve older homeless adults with basic needs and health, depression, and alcohol abuse problems (Cohen, Onserud, & Monaco, 1992). Cohen et al. found this innovative outreach program to be of vital importance in serving older homeless adults rarely reached by older adult services. In addition to providing respite, nutrition, medical, psychiatric treatment, and financial and vocational assistance, Project Rescue offers housing assistance. In direct contact with managers of substandard housing, Project Rescue staff are successful in obtaining shelter for older homeless adults, and legal services are provided to assist in preventing eviction. Results of this study stress the importance of outreach and continued contact to ensure successful outcomes in establishing stable housing arrangements.

Obtaining federal property for renovation into low-income housing is another viable possibility. The Interagency Council on the Homeless (Interagency Council, 1991) reports three types of properties available for the homeless through the federal government: real property, such as excess unused land and buildings; personal property, such as bedding, clothing, furniture, tools, and office equipment; and federally acquired foreclosed homes.

Depending on regulations, local government, housing authorities, and private nonprofit organizations are eligible to obtain this property. The purchaser is responsible for renovation (Interagency Council, 1991), and further assistance is available through various grant programs. The property is made available under Title V of the McKinney Act Federal Surplus Property Program (Interagency Council, 1991). Leases are usually for five years, with a five-year renewal option. If there is justification, Health and Human Services will consider up to a 20-year renewal. When the lease expires, the property, with improvements, belongs to the federal government.

Section 202 of the 1959 Housing Act was reinstated in 1974 within the Housing and Community Development Act. Since its inception, it has only produced 165,000 units, or 6000 apartments per year--not a serious attempt at affordable housing (Schwartz et al., 1988). This Act provides low-interest federal loans to nonprofit sponsors to construct or rehabilitate rental housing for older adults.

CONCLUSION

The housing situation for older homeless adults is unfortunate. Study after study shows housing to be the major priority, not only for shelter but for the therapeutic physical and mental effects this stabilizing environment provides. A recent report by the Special Committee on Aging shows that the housing needs of millions of older adults are not being addressed (Keigher et al., 1991). Because this group is more likely to be in old substandard housing, its needs in regard to service and shelter will increase tremendously in the near future.

It is no surprise that the problem in developing new programs is funding. Where state and federal government falls short in assistance, administrators must look to private, independent fund-raising efforts and private funds. Often administrators return a large portion of their own salaries into the renovation and running of homeless programs. Residents of housing projects take part in acquiring low-cost furniture and donate skills to the restoration of their homes.

As the older adult population increases, the danger of homelessness becomes imminent. Keigher and Pratt (1991) reported that from 1980 to 1985 households headed by adults age 65+ increased by 33 percent and those headed by adults age 75+ increased by 52 percent. Katsura, Struyk, and Newman (1989) extend this forecast to 2010, showing that the 65+ population will be approximately 39 million. This is a growth rate of 75 percent from 1985 and is a drastic contrast to the overall population growth rate of 32 percent. The population age 75+ will more than double to 19 million. Schwartz et al. (1988) predict that we will need 1.7 million new or rehabilitated units for the frail older adult, with necessary modifications to another 2 million existing units. It is crucial to follow two policy directions: (1) to provide enough housing; and (2) to provide health-care services for needy older adults to sustain independent living. Private industry will supply these services to older adults with means, but 3.5 million will need assistance (Schwartz et al., 1988). With appropriate housing facilities, another 300,000 older adults who are now in nursing homes could be added to the numbers now living independently.

Older adults are increasingly vulnerable to homelessness because of the growing shortage of low-income housing, federal housing program cutbacks, prepayment of federal mortgages on subsidized housing, gentrification, and the demolition of SROs. Ironically, the cost of caring for the homeless is far greater than the cost of providing decent housing. In addition, all services provided will not alleviate the problem of homelessness unless the nation adopts a federal policy of "housing for all" (Dluhy, 1990; Keigher et al., 1991). Government policy should *not* require homelessness as eligibility for services but should also direct funding to those at risk of homelessness. Homelessness, especially that of older adults, is an issue of growing concern. Fortunately, homeless policy is seen as a national priority by the Clinton Administration.

REFERENCES

Burt, Martha R. (1992). *Over the edge. The growth of homelessness in the 1980s*. Washington, DC: The Urban Institute Press.

Cohen, C. I., Onserud, H., & Monaco, C. (1992). Project Rescue: Serving the homeless and marginally housed elderly. *The Gerontologist*, *32*(4), 466-471.

Committee on Health Care for Homeless People. Institute of Medicine. (1988). *Homelessness, health, and human needs*. Washington, DC: National Academy Press.

Dluhy, M. J. (1990). Economics and public policies as factors in the rise of homelessness in South Florida. Cited in *The South Florida homelessness studies of 1989. A summary of key findings* (*Vol. 4*). Miami, FL: Barry University.

Doolin, J. (March/April, 1985). "America's untouchables": The elderly homeless. *Perspective on Aging*, pp. 8-11. Cited in *The new homeless crisis: Old and poor in the streets*. Hearing before the Select Committee on Aging, House of Representatives, Committee No. 101-784, September 26, 1990, pp. 96-99. Washington, DC.

Doolin, J. (1986). Planning for the special needs of the homeless elderly. *The Gerontologist*, *28*(3), 229-231.

The Harvard Mental Health Letter. (1990). Mental illness and homelessness: Part I. *7*(1), 1-4.

Hudson, B. A., Rauch, B. B., Dawson, G. D., Santos, J. F., & Burdick, D. C. (1990). *Homelessness: Special problems related to training, research, and the elderly*. Unpublished paper. University of Notre Dame, Department of Psychology, South Bend, IN.

Interagency Council on the Homeless, Council Communique. Special Edition (1991, July). *Obtaining federal property for the homeless: Questions and answers about federal property programs*. Washington, DC: HUD.

Katsura, H. M., Struyk, R. J., & Newman, S. J. (1989). *Housing for the elderly in 2010*. Washington, DC: The Urban Institute Press.

Keigher, S. M. (1991). The effects of a shrinking housing resource on older communities in Chicago. In S. M. Keigher (Ed.), *Housing risks and homelessness among the urban elderly* (pp. 93-110). New York: The Haworth Press.

Keigher, S. M., Berman, R. H., & Greenblatt S. T. (1991). The needs of older persons at risk of housing loss: Some conclusions and recommendations. In S.M. Keigher (Ed.), *Housing risks and homelessness among the urban elderly* (pp. 19-26). New York: The Haworth Press.

Keigher, S. M., & Greenblatt, S. T. (1992). Housing emergencies and the etiology of homelessness among the urban elderly. *The Gerontologist*, *32*(4), 457-465.

Keigher, S. M., & Pratt, F. (1991). Growing housing hardship among the elderly. In S. M. Keigher (Ed.), *Housing risks and homelessness among the urban elderly* (pp. 1-18). New York: The Haworth Press.

Levin, I. S., & Stockdill, J. W. (1984). Mentally ill and homeless: A national problem. In B. E. Jones (Ed.), *Treating the homeless: Urban psychiatry's challenge* (pp. 1-16). Washington, DC: American Psychiatric Press, Inc.

O'Connell, J. J., Summerfield, J., & Kellogg, F. R. (1990). The homeless elderly. In P. W. Brickner, L. K. Scharer, B. A. Conanan, M. Savarese, & B. C. Scanlan (Eds.), *Under the safety net: The health and social welfare of the homeless in the United States* (pp. 151-168). New York: W. W. Norton & Co.

Ovrebo, B., Minkler, M., & Liljestrand, P. (1991). No room at the inn: The disappearance of SRO housing in the United States. In S. M. Keigher (Ed.), *Housing risks and homelessness among the urban elderly* (pp. 77-92). New York: The Haworth Press.

Rossi, P. H. (1990). The old homeless and the new homelessness in historical perspective. *American Psychologist*, *45*(8), pp. 954-959.

Schwartz, D. C., Ferlauto, R. C., & Hoffman, D. N. (1988). *A new housing policy for America*. Philadelphia, PA: Temple University Press.

Tessler, R. C., & Dennis, D. L. (1989). *A synthesis of NIMH-funded research concerning persons who are homeless and mentally ill*. Program for the Homeless Mentally Ill. Division of Education and Service Systems Liason. Bethesda, MD: National Institute of Mental Health.

Torres-Gil, F. M. (1992). *The new aging*. New York: Auburn House.

U. S. Department of Housing and Urban Development (1994, April). 1995 Budget proposes doubling HUD homeless funds. *Community Development*, p. 1. Washington, DC: HUD, Office of Community Planning and Development.

What readers say about the homeless. (1994, April 24). *Parade Magazine*, p. 14.

Wiener, R. (1990, March/April). Prepayment hits countryside hard: ShelterForce. Cited in *The new homeless crisis: Old and poor in the streets*. Hearing before the Select Committee on Aging. House of Representatives, Committee No. 101-784, September 26, 1990, pp. 86-89. Washington, DC.

Wright, J. D. (1989). *Address unknown. The homeless in America*. New York: Aldine de Gruyter.

13

Housing Policy

Larry C. Mullins

Cogent public policy that concerns homeless persons in the United States presupposes that we know who the homeless are, what their needs are, how they can be helped, and the results of the help (i.e., the services and benefits they do receive). One way to begin to examine the policy-related issues that pertain to the homeless is to address the question, Who are the homeless? This question is difficult to answer because the face of homelessness is constantly changing, with current homeless including increasing numbers of families and older adults. The policies and attendant programs that relate to the homeless have to take into account the causes of homelessness.

A 1991 special issue of *American Psychologist* was devoted to concerns of the homeless in America and evolving policy priorities. Kondratas (1991) provides an overview and analysis of federal policies on homelessness, noting that homelessness is a social problem in need of redress, the causes of which are numerous and multifaceted.

DECLINE IN HOUSING

Kondratas states that "over the past few decades, there has been a significant decline in the number of housing units available to low-income persons, and the poor are paying increasingly higher proportions of their income in rents" (1991, p. 1228). The question is why. It is argued by many that this condition is the result of Reagan-era housing budget cuts from what had been authorized under the Carter Administration. However, this does not seem to be the case because (1) the actual expenditures for housing in the two administrations were much the same; and (2) the number of federally subsidized, low-income units actually increased in the early to mid-1980s, at a time when homelessness had become a national issue. What explains the reduction in housing for the poor? It has been argued by Moore (1990) that the decline in housing stock for those with low income is not the result of federal budget cuts but the result of losses due to such things as urban renewal, inflation-driven housing speculation, rent control, gentrification, tax policies, and exclusionary zoning.

Politically, the cause of homelessness was presumed to be the result of housing budget cuts and other housing-related policies in combination with increased unemployment, decreased income, and a reduction in social support programs. Indeed, Barancik (1989) points out that between 1981 and 1989, federal housing programs for the poor were cut by approximately 75 percent, even though such programs were never adequate at optimal funding to meet the needs of even the eligible poor. By 1989, there were two-year waiting lists for federal housing programs (Foscarinis, 1991), with such long waiting lists in 67 percent of 27 major cities that the waiting lists were closed.

Concurrent with these developments, urban redevelopment projects as early as 1970 led to the elimination of low-income housing in the private sector (Wright & Lam, 1987). In fact, between 1970 and 1980 about half of the nation's SRO units were destroyed (Hopper & Hamberg, 1986). This led to the displacement of thousands of American poor (Hartman, 1988). Unfortunately, there were no provisions for replacement housing. The poor have been squeezed out of the housing market into shelters or onto the streets (Shapiro, 1989).

CUTS IN SOCIAL SERVICES

Rossi (1989) points out that as the supply of affordable housing shrank, social service relief programs also were being slashed. Thus, those who were most vulnerable with respect to housing were increasingly likely not to have other social support services on which they could depend. This reflected the general downturn in the American economy over the past decade. Foscarinis (1991) states bluntly, "For the poorest of the poor, facing decreasing resources and rising housing costs, homelessness was the predictable result" (pp. 1233-1234).

In the late 1980s, it was recognized that homelessness was a problem that resulted from multiple causes and needed a long-term structural solution rather than a short-term fix. This recognition resulted in the Stewart B. McKinney Homeless Assistance Act of 1987 (Public Law 100-77). "The McKinney Act was the first piece of federal legislation to recognize the multiple and longer term needs of the homeless and to recognize that homelessness is far more than a housing problem. The act comprises some 20 programs, administered by seven federal departments, and provides not only housing assistance but also health and mental health care, food assistance, substance-abuse treatment, education, and job training" (Kondratas, 1991, p. 1228).

Unfortunately, the McKinney Act has been less effective than expected for several reasons: It was not fully funded between 1987 and 1990; it received less than requested in 1991, and the system remained fragmented (Kondratas, 1991).

FUTURE DIRECTIONS

Finding solutions to homelessness has become a national priority. Henry Cisneros, Secretary of HUD, recognized in a recent report (U. S. Housing and Urban Development, 1993) the need for redressing the housing and community development needs for those with low and moderate income. He indicated in the preface to this report that five operational priorities will guide policy: "reducing the number of homeless Americans, making public housing a source of community pride; expanding housing opportunities for low or moderate income people; opening housing markets to minorities; and empowering communities" (U. S. Housing and Urban Development, 1993, p. 5).

The Clinton Administration 1995 budget proposal requests increased funding for the McKinney programs--Shelter Grant, Supportive Housing, Shelter Plus Care, Section 8 Moderate Rehabilitation Single Room Occupancy, Safe Haven, and Rural Homeless programs. It is also proposed that the Emergency Food and Shelter Program be transferred to HUD and that five-year Section 8 certificates be provided to assist previously homeless families to obtain permanent housing in the private market (U. S. Housing and Urban Development, 1994).

The federal plan to end homelessness provides a framework for comprehensive federal action in concert with public and private efforts to help end the tragedy of homelessness. The goals and objectives follow (U.S. Housing and Urban Development, 1992, p. 27).

Goals

The federal plan's goals are to reduce homelessness by improving the coordination and delivery of assistance designed to (1) help homeless families and individuals obtain appropriate permanent housing and become as self-sufficient as possible, and (2) prevent others from becoming homeless.

Objectives

1. *Define needs of homeless subgroups.* Provide clear descriptions of the needs that typically must be met for members of each subgroup of the homeless population to move out of homelessness.
2. *Improve coordination among federal, state, private, and voluntary homelessness efforts.* Improve the coordination of federal, state, and local public and private efforts through comprehensive federal, state, and local strategies for providing assistance to the homeless. Ensure that these measures go beyond emergency measures and include longer-term mechanisms designed to address the fundamental problems that lead to homelessness.
3. *Increase homeless participation in mainstream programs.* Increase participation of homeless families and individuals in programs that, although not specifically targeted toward homelessness, provide income support, social services, health care, education, employment, and housing. Monitor and evaluate these programs' impact on homelessness and increase data collection relating to homeless participation in them.
4. *Improve homelessness-targeted programs.* Review the McKinney Act and other programs specifically targeted to assist the homeless. This review will help identify changes that can be made to improve the efficiency and effectiveness of these programs in addressing the multiple and diverse needs of the various subgroups of homeless persons.
5. *Increase availability of support services in combination with housing.* Take actions to increase the availability of necessary support services and ensure that these services are provided in combination with appropriate housing. Ensure that homeless families with children receive appropriate supportive housing rather than being housed in welfare hotels.
6. *Improve access to permanent housing.* Take actions to improve the accessibility of decent, affordable, and permanent housing to homeless families and individuals.
7. *Develop strategies for preventing homelessness.* Improve methods of identifying families and individuals clearly at risk of imminent homelessness; identify and propose changes in current policies that may be contributing to homelessness; and propose other initiatives to help prevent these persons from becoming homeless.
8. *Increase knowledge of how best to address homelessness.* Through increased data collection, research, and evaluation,

improve understanding of the needs of homeless families and individuals, how well those needs are being met by current activities, and how better to meet those current needs in the future. Widely disseminate this information to help improve policies and practices and to educate the public on homelessness and what is being done across the country to help.

SUMMARY

In finding long-term solutions for homelessness, Foscarinis (1991) suggests a strategy rooted in public pressure on government representatives. Her strategy proposes education about the condition of the homeless and up-to-date information on proposed legislative action; contact with government representatives; and exertion of political pressure by professional organizations in a manner which increases the likelihood of action.

REFERENCES

Barancik, S. (1989). *Poverty rate and household income stalemate as rich-poor gap hits post-war high.* Washington, DC: Center on Budget and Policy Priorities.

Foscarinis, M. (1991). The politics of homelessness: A call to action. *American Psychologist*, *46*, 1232-1238.

Hartman, C. (1988). Decent, affordable housing for all. In M. Raskin & C. Hartman (Eds.), *Winning America* (pp. 190-200). Boston: South End Press.

Hopper, K., & Hamberg, J. (1986). The making of America's homeless: From skid row to new poor: 1945-1984. In R. G. Bratt, C. Hartman, & A. Meyerson (Eds.), *Critical perspectives on housing* (pp. 12-40). Philadelphia, PA: Temple University Press.

Kondratas, A. (1991). Ending homelessness: Policy challenges. *American Psychologist*, *46*, 1226-1231.

Moore, C. C. (1990). *Housing policy in New York: Myth and reality.* Washington, DC: Cato Institute.

Rossi, P. (1989). *Down and out in America.* Chicago: University of Chicago Press.

Shapiro, I. (1989). *Laboring for less.* Washington, D.C.: Center on Budget and Policy Priorities.

U. S. Department of Housing and Urban Development (1992, September). *Federal progress towards ending homelessness: 1991-92 Annual report of the Interagency Council on the Homeless.* p. 27. Washington, D.C.: HUD.

U. S. Department of Housing and Urban Development. (1993, October). *Creating communities of change: Priorities of U.S. Department of Housing and Urban Development*. Executive Summary. Washington, D.C.: HUD.

U. S. Department of Housing and Urban Development. (1994, April). 1995 Budget proposes doubling HUD homeless funds. *Community Connections*. p. 1. Washington, DC: HUD, Office of Community Development.

Wright, J. D. & Lam, J. A. (1987). Homelessness and the low-income housing supply. *Social Policy*, *17*, 49-53.

14

Concluding Thoughts

Diane Wiatt Rich and Thomas A. Rich

Foscarinis (1991) reminds us that homelessness is not merely a *problem*. "It is human beings living on the streets, eating out of garbage cans, and dressing in rags. It is desperate need amid overwhelming abundance. And each year, it is death in the streets" (p. 1236). All homeless people have certain things in common: the need for food, clothing, shelter, health care, income (job, pension, etc.), and a sense of worth. Community caregivers struggle with limited resources to meet these needs, often with little left to assist the individual in his or her uniqueness. Homelessness has multiple causes, and the individuals only appear homogeneous when seen from their survival needs.

Approaches to meet and respect individual uniqueness must go beyond labels, stereotypes, and hostile views. Broad categories may be useful for demographics but do not describe the myriad cause-and-effect relationships. Even in this book we discuss older homeless adults as one group, but the age groups 50 to 62 and 62+ become two new groups with different service needs.

The face of the homeless is frequently clouded by results of studies conducted in different geographic areas and in agencies serving different populations. Viewing the homeless as people with individual needs leads us in two directions. First, there should be a national study of the homeless with sample size and characteristics selected so that individual target groups can be identified and receive focused attention for prevention and intervention. Second, there must be follow-through on HUD's new plan, *Priority: Home! The Federal Plan to Break the Cycle of Homelessness* (U.S. Housing and Urban Development, 1994) which recognizes "that it [homelessness] is larger in scale than previously recognized and involves people suffering from both *chronic disabilities* as well as *crisis poverty*" (p. 1).

Maslow's (1970) concept of a hierarchy of needs--physiological, safety, love and belonging, esteem, and self-actualization--providesa framework for planning services as well as for viewing the unique needs of homeless individuals. For a variety of reasons, agencies have focused on meeting the physiological and safety needs of the homeless. The new emphasis by HUD on a continuum of care offers communities the opportunity to provide interventions which meet both the physiological and safety needs and the higher-level needs of homeless people.

REFERENCES

Foscarinis, M. (1991). The politics of homelessness: A call to action. *American Psychologist*, *46*, 1232-1238.

Maslow, A.H. (1970). *Motivation and personality* (2nd ed.). New York: Harper & Row.

U. S. Department of Housing and Urban Development. (1994, May). Priority number one: Help the homeless. *Community Connections*, p. 1. Washington, DC: HUD, Office of Community Development.

Appendix

Old and Homeless in Tampa Bay: A Survey

Thomas A. Rich, Louisette A. Boucher, and Diane Wiatt Rich

In 1991, a survey of older homeless adults in Pinellas and Hillsborough counties (Tampa Bay area) was conducted. The subjects were interviewed in a wide variety of community agencies providing services for the homeless. The purpose of this survey was to provide a better understanding of the homeless in this region and to guide the development of effective instructional materials for a better understanding of older homeless adults.

The field survey was administered by clinicians from the Mature Adult Counseling Center of the Florida Mental Health Institute, University of South Florida. Interviewing was conducted in homeless shelters and agencies throughout the seven-day week, both at night and in the daytime to provide the widest possible range of subjects. The survey instrument was a composite of several clinical instruments currently used in local agencies and designed specifically for homeless adults. The survey included basic background information on reasons for being homeless, attitudes about being homeless, mental health, and other aspects of homelessness.

THE SAMPLE

One hundred and three older homeless adults (OHA) were identified and interviewed through their use of services in the homeless networks in the Tampa Bay area. The services received are shown in Table A.1, and numbers show that many clients are receiving multiple services. Obtaining food either by receiving prepared meals or receiving food that they can prepare themselves is a high priority. The next four services in order of importance are assistance with clothing, transitional housing, emergency shelter, and emergency health care. Fifteen percent report working in a labor pool and 6.8 percent report employment assistance. The major services requested are for survival assistance and are not rehabilitative in emphasis.

Table A.1
Services Received (*N* = 103)

Services	Percentage Receiving Services
Assistance with meals	89.3
Assistance with clothing	60.2
Assistance with food	32.0
Transitional housing	24.3
Emergency shelter	23.3
Emergency health care	15.5
Labor pool	14.6
Day shelter	12.6
Primary health care	10.7
Mental health counseling	10.7
Employment assistance	6.8
Assistance with transportation	6.8
Assistance with rent	2.9
Education/training	1.9
Childcare	1.0
Permanent housing	1.0
Assistance with utilities	0.0
Other assistance	3.9

The respondents' living situations (Table A.2) may be the basis for the priorities observed in services needed. Almost 38 percent report living outside, on the street, or in parks, whereas 30 percent live in a self-defined or named shelter. Transitional or temporary housing (such as with friends or family, in cars, vans, or trucks, or in vacant buildings) is reported by 32 percent of the respondents. Living on the street was primarily by choice, with dislike of shelters based on rules and regulations, crowding, and a general feeling of loss of freedom.

Table A.2
Living Situation (N = 103)

Location	Percentage
Outside, street, park	37.9
Shelter	30.1
Transitional housing	10.7
Own room or apartment	7.8
With friends or family	5.8
Car, van, or truck	5.8
Vacant building	1.9

When asked about their reasons for being homeless (Table A.3), the anticipated answer is that they cannot afford rent or rent deposits. These are followed by alcohol abuse and loss of job, illness, and a range of other reasons, such as being divorced or abandoned by spouse or family, mental illness, drug abuse, and loss of home.

Table A.3
Reasons for Homelessness (N = 103)

Reasons	Percentage
Cannot afford rent	75.7
Cannot afford deposit	68.0
Alcohol abuse	37.9
Lost job	35.0
Sick and unable to work	28.2
Left adult family	14.6
Newly released from jail/legal problems	8.7
Newly released from hospital	7.8
Divorce	7.8
Abandoned by spouse/family	6.8
Asked by family/friends to leave	6.8
Mental illness	4.9
Drug abuse	4.9
Prefers street life	3.9
Home foreclosed	2.9
Home condemned	2.9
Spouse abuse	1.9
Fire, flood, etc.	1.0
Other	15.5

The homeless in the Tampa Bay area are not unlike the rest of Florida in that they have come to the area from a variety of other states. The largest number are from Florida and/or the Tampa Bay area, with the next largest number coming from southern states followed by northern and midwest states and a scattering from other areas. A few report coming to the Tampa Bay area directly from the military (Table A.4). They have been in the local area from one month or less to over six years, with 40 percent being in the over six-year category as long-time residents of this area (Table A.5). The majority of this sample have been homeless from two months to four years, with about 22 percent homeless for a longer period (Table A.6). Again, these figures point out the heterogeneity of the sample, with people who have become homeless in the fairly recent past and those who have adjusted to street life over several years.

Table A.4
Location before Tampa Bay (*N* = 100)

Region	Percentage
Florida	30.4
South	28.0
North	17.0
Midwest	15.0
West	6.0
Military	4.0

Table A.5
Length of Time in County (*N* = 103)

Months	Percentage
1 month or less	16.5
02 to 12 months	22.3
13 to 48 months	13.6
49 to 72 months	7.8
73 plus months	39.8

Table A.6
Length of Time Since Last Permanent Residence (*N* = 100)

Months	Percentage
1 month or less	8.0
02 to 12 months	42.0
13 to 48 months	28.0
49 to 72 months	5.0
73 plus months	17.0

HOW DO THEY FEEL ABOUT BEING HOMELESS?

Being homeless is closely related to isolation and loneliness. Sixty-two percent of the sample indicate that they have no close associates (Table A.7). Twenty-six percent report having some friends, but these are usually street friends, and a smaller percentage have some connection with their family. When asked about other major problems and concerns experienced by the homeless (Table A.8), lack of job, shelter, and money are major concerns. Safety also seems to be a major problem, and 5 percent report that they want off the streets. Some are aware that aging exacerbates the problem of being on the street.

Table A.7
Close Associates (*N* = 103)

Associates	Percentage
None	62.1
Friends	26.2
Family	6.8
Family & Friends	4.9

Table A.8
Major Problems and Concerns Experienced as Homeless (*N* = 103)

Problems and concerns	Percentage
Job	25.2
Shelter	22.3
Money	16.5
Safety	13.6
Cleanliness	10.7
Alcohol	9.7
Food	9.7
Health & medical insurance	8.7
No problems or concerns	7.8
Wanting off the streets	4.9
Basic necessities	4.9
Age	2.9
Staying warm	1.9
Loneliness	1.9
Gas for car	0.9
Transportation	0.9

When asked about the advantages of being homeless, 77.5 percent said there are none, but a smaller group, 13.7 percent, indicated that they liked the lack of responsibility and saw some other advantages to being on the street (Table A.9).

Table A.9
Advantages to Being Homeless (*N* = 102)

Advantages	Percentage
None	77.5
No responsibility	13.7
Other advantages	8.8

Survival strengths (Table A.10) were also questioned, with 37 percent reporting determination and a will to survive as their strengths, followed very closely by 26 percent who referred to religious beliefs. A few indicated that they had no survival strengths, while others had no answer. Some, because of small physical size and age, see themselves at a distinct disadvantage on the streets. When asked about personal weaknesses that make survival more difficult (Table A.11), 37 percent indicated that they had none, but others listed in rank order alcohol, physical health problems, age, and physical size.

Table A.10
Survival Strengths (*N* = 99)

Strengths	Percentage
Determination and will to survive	37.4
Religion	26.3
Street smarts	19.2
Other than above	12.1
None	5.1

Table A.11
Personal Weaknesses That Make Survival More Difficult (*N* = 98)

Weaknesses	Percentage
None	36.7
Alcohol	18.4
Physical health problems	12.2
Age	6.1
Physical size	3.1
Other than above	23.5

THE DEMOGRAPHY OF HOMELESS PERSONS

For this study, based on the generally accepted age in the literature, older homelessness was defined as age 50+. Research indicates that homeless adults over 50 may be considered old because of stresses, nutritional problems, untreated health conditions, etc. In this sample, the age range was from 50 to 84, with a mean age of 57.5 and a median age of 56.0 (Table A.12). In addition, 85 percent are males and 15 percent females, with 70 percent white, 26 percent black, and 4 percent Hispanics (Tables A.13, A.14). In Table A.15, marital status is shown, with the highest percentage (46 percent) divorced, while few (3.9 percent) are still married. Consistent with other information, the respondents are alone.

Table A.12
Age of Respondents (*N* = 103)

Age range	Percentage
50 to 55	47.6
56 to 60	25.2
61 to 65	16.5
66 to 70	4.9
71 to 75	4.8
76 to 85	1.0

Mean: 57.5 Median: 56.0 Mode: 54.0

Table A.13
Sex (*N* = 103)

Sex	Percentage
Male	85.4
Female	14.6

Table A.14
Race/Ethnic Background (*N* = 103)

Race/ethnicity	Percentage
White	69.9
Black	26.2
Hispanic - Mexican	2.9
Other Hispanics	1.0

Table A.15
Marital Status (N = 103)

Marital status	Percentage
Divorced	45.6
Never married	28.2
Widowed	13.6
Separated	8.7
Married	3.9

Responses to religious affiliation show that the majority, 60 percent, are Protestant, with 17.5 percent Catholic and 28 percent reporting other religions or no religion (Table A.16). Educationally, they represent a wide range. A small percentage have very little education, 0 to 3 years of schooling, with about 22 percent reporting education of 13 or more years (Table A.17). As shown in Table A.18, 34 percent report nonskilled occupations. Skilled workers represent 46 percent of the sample; clerical, sales, and professional workers represent 15 percent; and 6 percent had been in military service. Many of these individuals have held responsible positions in the past but apparently no longer have the necessary skills or stability for employment. When asked about days of work in the last 30 days, almost 84 percent indicated that they had had no employment (Table A.19).

Table A.16
Religious Affiliations (N = 103)

Denomination	Percentage
Protestant	60.2
Catholic	17.5
Jewish	1.0
Other	21.4
None	6.8

Table A.17
Education (N = 103)

School	Percentage
0 to 3	5.8
4 to 9	27.2
10 to 12	45.6
13 to 15	14.6
16 and more	6.8

Table A.18
Major Past Occupation (N = 103)

Type of occupation	Percentage
Nonskilled	34.3
Skilled	45.6
Clerical	7.8
Sales	3.9
Professional	2.9
Service (military)	5.8

Table A.19
Days Worked in the Last 30 Days (N = 103)

Number of days	Percentage
None	83.5
1 to 4 days	6.8
5 to 8 days	2.0
9 to 12 days	1.0
13 to 16 days	1.0
17 to 20 days	2.9
21 days	1.0

Sixty-seven percent of subjects report no income, and 19 percent report income from $3,000 to over $10,000 (Table A.20). Income seems to rise sharply after age 65, when retirement funds, particularly Social Security, become operational. As shown in Table A.21, the most frequent income source is Social Security, which is received by 8.7 percent of the sample, followed by wages, Supplemental Security Income, VA income, and private pensions. Some individuals have sufficient income to suggest that they could be financially independent and off the street. The age/income relationship suggests that a group of older homeless adults age 60 and over may be a target group for intervention since retirement income (i.e., Social Security, pensions, and eligibility for Older Americans Act services) is reached.

Table A.20
Income (N = 103)

Income range	Percentage
None	67.0
$1 to	13.6
3000 to	6.8
5200 to	6.8
7800 to	5.8

Table A.21
Source of Income (N = 103)

Sources	Percentage
None	67.0
Social Security Administration	8.7
Wages	6.8
Supplemental Security Income	3.9
Veterans Administration	2.9
Private pensions	2.9
Other	7.8

PHYSICAL HEALTH STATUS

The majority of the older adults in this sample do not have health insurance (Table A.22), although some of the older ones are now eligible for Medicare and Medicaid. When asked about a last medical examination, 57 percent said that they have had one within the last year and 14 percent within the last two years, and some do not remember how long ago (Table A.23). They are not clear about where these medical exams or screenings took place or about the results.

Table A.22
Health Insurance (N = 103)

Insurance	Percentage
None	81.6
Medicare	8.7
Medicaid	3.9
Other	3.9
Private insurance	1.0
More than one listed	1.0

Table A.23
Last Medical Exam (N = 101)

Time Period	Percentage
Within the last year	57.3
Within the last 2 years	13.6
More than 2 years ago	15.5
Did not remember how long ago	11.7

Table A.24 reports average height and weight, but this is useful mostly for comparison for loss or gain of weight or for the perception of small size being a danger on the streets. The majority report two meals or fewer per day, which suggests some nutritional problems (Table A.25). Sleeping patterns (Table A.26) show slightly over 50 percent sleeping through the night, with others waking intermittently or having difficulty going to sleep.

Table A.24
Average Height and Weight (*N* = 103)

Race & sex	Percentage	Ht	Range	Wt	Range
White males	57.3	5'8"	5'1" to 6'	161.9	110 to 250
Black males	26.2	5'9"	5'1" to 6'3"	164.3	118 to 215
White	12.6	5'5"	5'2" to 5'9"	146.6	107 to 200
Other males	1.9	5'8"	5'6" to 5'9"	152.5	150 to 155
Other females	1.9	5'4"	5'2" to 5'6"	168.0	156 to 180
Black females	0.0	--	--	--	--

Table A.25
Meals per Day (*N* = 103)

Number	Percentage
3 meals per day	25.2
2 meals per day	48.5
1 meal per day	25.2
Less than 1 meal per day	1.0

Table A.26
Sleeping Pattern (*N* = 102)

Quality of Sleep	Percentage
Sleeps through the night	52.9
Awakens intermittently	21.6
Difficulty going to sleep	16.7
Wakes up early and can't go back to sleep	5.9
Sleeps too much	62.0
Other problems	1.0

Medical symptoms reported (Table A.27) indicate dental problems as the most frequently reported problem. It appears that this is where the least treatment is available or where treatment requires a long waiting time. Dental problems are followed by alcohol and drug abuse concerns, vision problems, blood pressure, asthma and shortness of breath, weight loss or gain, and chronic cough and headaches. Many of these symptoms reflect what would be expected of an older population and also suggest the problems for this sample. Care for chronic disease is clearly needed, although the most available care reported is emergency care.

Table A.27
Medical Symptoms (*N* = 103)

Symptoms	Frequency
Dental problems	49.5
Alcohol/drug abuse	38.8
Eye problems	34.0
Blood pressure problems	27.2
Asthma and shortness of breath	23.3
Weight loss or gain	21.4
Chronic cough	21.4
Frequent or severe headache	20.4
Hearing problems	16.5
Dizziness or fainting spells	14.6
Change in memory/concentration	14.6
Palpitations	12.6
Heart trouble	11.7
Stomach/bowel problems	7.8
Epilepsy/seizure	6.8
Urine sugar/albumin	3.9
Frequent/painful urination	3.9
Venereal disease	3.9
Stroke symptoms	2.9
Contagious disease	2.9
Jaundice/liver problems	1.9
Paralysis	1.0
Loss of limb	1.0
Neurological/thyroid problems	0.0

Only 33 percent of the respondents reported taking medications. If we compare the medications taken (Table A.28) with the medical symptoms reported (Table A.27), we can identify an inappropriate rate of treatment. For example, 23 percent report asthma and shortness of breath, but only 6 percent report taking medication for respiratory problems. This can also be seen for cardiovascular problems--39 percent report blood pressure problems and heart trouble, and only 20 percent are on a medication regimen.

Table A.28
Medications Taken at Present (N = 34)

Name		Percentage
Cardiovascular drugs		20.4
Psychotropic drugs		10.7
Antidepressants	4.9	
Sleeping pills	2.9	
Other	2.9	
Tranquilizers	0.0	
Anti-inflammatory		9.7
Respiratory drugs		5.8
Gastrointestinal drugs		3.9
Antibiotics		2.9
Vitamins		2.9
Hypoglycemics		1.9
Antabuse		1.0
Weight control drug		0.0

BEHAVIORAL AND PHYSICAL PROBLEMS

A major problem on the streets is that of alcohol usage. Fifty-four percent of those in the sample report alcohol usage (Table A.29A). When one looks further at those who currently drink alcohol (Table A.29B), 8 percent drink 2 to 10 drinks per day and 52 percent drink 11 or more drinks per day, suggesting alcohol problems for about 30 or 40 percent in this sample. The drink of preference appears to be beer, reported by both current and former drinkers, with hard liquor and wine following (Tables A.29C and D).

Table A.29A
Alcohol Usage (N = 103)

Pattern	Percentage
Alcohol users	54.4
Former	31.1
Never drank	14.6

Table A.29B
Daily Drinking Pattern: Alcohol Users (N = 56)

Number of drinks	Percentage
1 or less	8.9
2 to 10	7.5
11 or more	51.8
No answer	1.8

Table A.29C
Past Alcohol Usage of Former Drinkers (N = 32)

Number of drinks	Percentage
1 or less	15.6
2 to 10	12.5
11 or more (dependency)	71.9

Table A.29D
Type of Alcohol Used: Current and Former Drinkers (N = 88)

Type	Percentage
Beer	46.0
Hard liquor	17.2
Wine	8.0
Any combination of above	28.7

In Table A.30A, 53 percent report smoking a pack of cigarettes a day, 24 percent two packs a day, and 2 percent three packs a day. Combined with alcohol, this indicates another significant health risk for older adults on the street. When we look at smoking history (Table A.30B), only 22.9 percent of the sample population are non-smokers. Most have been smoking for many years (some as long as 60 years) and apparently have little incentive or motivation to stop smoking while on the streets.

Table A.30A
Smoking Pattern (N = 102)

Packs	Percentage
None	21.6
1 pack	53.0
2 packs	23.5
3 packs	2.0

Table A.30B
Smoking History (N = 101)

Years	Percentage
0	22.8
1 to 3	0.0
4 to 10	4.0
11 to 15	4.0
16 to 20	4.0
21 to 25	3.0
26 to 30	14.9
31 to 35	7.0
36 to 40	16.8
41 to 45	12.9
46 to 50	7.9
51 to 55	2.0
55 to 60	1.0

The street drug usage in this age group as reported is quite small with 7 persons (6.8 percent) indicating that they use drugs on a daily basis or when they can get them, such as biweekly (Tables A.31A, A.31B). They have been using drugs for several years, and some are long-term drug users (Table A.31C), with the type of drug being primarily cocaine, crack, and other unspecified drugs (Table A.31B).

Table A.31A
Street Drug Pattern (N = 103)

Usage	Percentage
Yes	6.8
No	93.2

Table A.31B
Frequency of Drug Usage (N = 7)

Frequency	Percentage
Daily usage	57.1
Weekly usage	28.6
Bi-weekly	1.0

Table A.31C
History of Drug Use (N = 7)

Years	Percentage
1 to 5 years	28.6
6 to 10 years	42.9
10 to 20 years	14.3
20 to 30 years	14.3

Table A.31 D
Types of Drugs Used (N = 7)

Drugs	Percentage
Cocaine	28.6
Crack	42.9
Other	28.6

MENTAL HEALTH

The general appearance of older homeless adults reflects their economic, psychological, and social status. The clinicians interviewing the sample viewed about 45 percent as looking normal in general appearance (Table A.32). The other 55 percent presented a different appearance due to a variety of factors, including abnormal dress, attitude appearing strange, motor activity seen as abnormal, mood states, affect, and, in some cases, thought content or thought form. Judgment was rated as good 27 percent of the time, and only 33 percent were seen as having good insight into their problems. Generally speaking, orientation to time, place, and person, as well as immediate memory, was fairly good.

Table A.32
Mental Status (*N* = 103)

Characteristics	Percentage		
	Normal	Abnormal	
General appearance	44.7	55.3	
Dress	78.6	21.4	
Attitude	82.5	17.5	
Motor activity	81.6	18.4	
Mood	46.6	53.4	
Affect	93.2	6.8	
Thought form	68.0	32.0	
Thought content	86.4	13.6	
Behavior patterns	56.3	43.7	
	Poor	Fair	Good
Judgment	23.3	49.5	27.2
Insight into problems	22.3	44.7	33.0
	Poor	Fair	Intact
Orientation to persons			100.0
Orientation to place	1.9		98.1
Orientation to time	1.0		99.0
Immediate memory	1.9	7.8	90.3
Recent memory	1.9	5.8	92.2
Remote memory	1.0	2.9	96.1

Table A.33 shows that 27 percent report hospitalization for alcohol problems, 4 percent for mental health problems, and 2 percent for dual diagnoses. It is likely that there is some underreporting for these latter two categories. When asked about the presence of mental health problems (Table A.34), 19 percent report participation in a mental health program at some point in their lives, 20 percent report a mental health hospitalization, and a small percentage report visual and auditory hallucinations, obsessive or confused thoughts, or just feeling emotionally ill. Almost 14 percent report past suicidal behavior, with about 9 percent reporting past assaultive or homicidal behavior. Figures for present suicidal or assaultive behavior are much smaller (Table A.35).

Table A.33
Mental Health Hospitalization Reported (*N* = 103)

Types	Percentage
Alcohol problems	26.2
Mental health problems	3.9
Dual diagnosis	1.9
No hospitalization	68.0

Table A.34
Presence of Mental Health Problems (*N* = 103)

Types of problems	Yes	Percentage
1. Participation in mental health program	20	19.4
2. Self-report of mental health	21	20.4
3. Visual and auditory hallucinations	5	4.9
4. Expressed false beliefs	0	0.0
5. Expressed being controlled	0	0.0
6. Mood shifts during interview	2	1.9
7. Obsessive or confused thoughts	8	7.8
8. Feels emotionally ill	19	18.4

Table A.35
Suicidal Behavior (*N* = 101)

Present behavior	Percentage
None	72.3
Past suicidal behavior	13.9
Past assaultive/homicidal behavior	8.9
Present suicidal ideation	3.0
Present assaultive/homicidal behavior	2.0

From the provisional diagnostic impression of *DSM-III-R*, Axis I (the clinicians rarely rated Axis II because of the brevity of the interview), 24 percent were diagnosed with an absence of mental health problems (Table A.36). Alcohol dependency was diagnosed in 36 percent of the sample and drug dependency in 2 percent, and 25 percent were diagnosed with depression/dysthymic disorder. The remainder of the diagnoses seemed to be scattered, with typical problems for this age population, with one exception. Based on different sources in the literature, there seems to be a much lower report of dementia or schizophrenia than found in other studies.

Table A.36
Provisional Diagnostic Impression DSM-III-R, Axis I (N = 103)

Diagnostic	No.	Percentage
Absence of mental health problem	25	24.3
Alcohol dependency	37	35.9
Drug dependency	2	1.9
Alcohol & drug dependency	2	1.9
Major depression--dysthymic disorder	26	25.2
Rule out OBS/Schizophrenia	5	4.9
Bereavement	1	1.0
Malingering	1	1.0
Anxiety	1	1.0
Phase of life	1	1.0
Adjustment disorders	2	1.9

The Global Assessment of Functioning (GAF) on the current level is shown in Table A.37. Since the Global Assessment of Functioning considers psychological, social, and occupational functioning, this would indicate that 88 percent show moderate to serious symptoms that result in impaired functioning and probably represents a need for treatment not currently being received. On the other end of the scale, 12 percent could be seen as functioning in a reasonably adequate manner with mild to minimal symptoms and problems.

Table A.37
Current Global Assessment of Functioning--GAF (N = 103)

Scale	Number	Percentage
90 to 81	0	0.0
80 to 71	2	2.0
70 to 61	10	9.8
60 to 51	11	10.7
50 to 41	30	36.9
40 to 31	35	34.0
30 to 21	5	4.8
20 to 11	2	1.9

Mean 46.31 Std. dev. 11.09 Min. 20 Max. 80

Index

advocacy, 85, 93
ageism, 7, 40
AIDS, 33, 41, 48
alcoholism. *See* substance abuse
Alzheimer's Disease, 24-25
anemia, 41, 43, 62
anxiety, 12, 24, 70-71
arthritis, 41, 47-49

boredom, 30

caffeine, 72
caregivers, 26
case management, 14, 19, 21, 37, 85
case studies, 93-96
chronic pain, 24
cocaine, 34, 72
Community Mental Health Centers Act of 1962, 20
community resources, 14, 83, 91-100; innovative approaches, 20-21, 50, 96-100, 106-7
continuity of care, 14, 67, 80, 118
crime, 105

deinstitutionalization, 11-12, 18, 105
delirium, 23, 70, 71
dementia, 23-24
demographics, 9, 11-13, 18-19, 103-5, 125-28, 117-18
dental problems, 49, 87, 130
depression, 12, 23-26, 41, 43, 68-69
diabetes, 41, 48, 57-58
diuretics, 62
dual diagnosis, 19, 34, 40

economics, 11, 101-2, 105-6
education, 8, 14, 59, 84-85, 87
employment/unemployment, 14, 19, 127-28
empowerment, 79-88
entitlements, 84
eye disorders, 41

Farmer's Home Administration, 102-3
frostbite, 48

hallucinations, 61, 70
hearing impairments, 58
heat stroke, 41, 70
hepatitis, 41
HIV, 33, 41, 48
homeless coalitions, 14, 93
homeless history, 2-4
homeless people's views of street life, 11-12, 30, 49-50, 93-96, 100; advantages/disadvantages to being homeless, 124; survival strengths, 124
homelessness defined, 1, 18, 117
housing, 37-38, 84, 87, 101-8, 111-15; deinstitutionalization, 11-12, 18, 105; future directions, 113-15; policy, 101-8, 111-15
Housing Act of 1987, 103
HUD, 13, 20, 54, 96, 103, 106, 113-15, 117-18
hypertension, 41, 43, 48, 58

income tax, 86
insomnia, 43, 71
isolation, 81

Kansas vagrancy statute of 1889, 3

labels, 1, 4, 117. *See also* stereotypes
law enforcement, 83
loneliness, 23, 30

malnutrition, 48, 49, 63
Maslow, A.H., 118
medical problems, 48-49
Medicare, 4
medication, 53-63, 65-75, 131, compliance, 56-59, 66-68; side effects, 60-63
mental health, 12, 17-21, 23-26, 134-37

nutrition, 24, 47

osteoporosis, 48
outreach, 19, 20, 37, 79-88

poisoning, 73-75
Poor Law Act of 1601, 2
Protestant Reformation, 2
psychotropic medications, 47, 65-75; compliance, 66-68; side effects, 72-75

referral, 23
respiratory illnesses, 48, 49

safety, 81
schizophrenia, 23, 70, 73
Section 8 housing, 106
sexually transmitted diseases, 41
shelters, 17, 79, 83
Single Resident Occupancies. *See* SROs
skid row, 3
sleeping problems, 23
Social Security, 4, 12, 18, 19, 127-28
SROs, 104-5, 108, 112
SSI, 19, 127
stereotypes, 7-9, 31. *See also* labels
Stewart B. McKinney Homeless Assistance Act of 1987, 18-19, 107, 112-14
stress, 23, 47, 48, 84
substance abuse, 12, 18, 24, 29-44, 64, 132-37; treatment, 37-40, 42-44, 124, 131-33
suicide, 73-75

Tampa Bay survey, 12, 66, 119-37
thermoregulation, 41, 47, 72-73
transitional housing, 20, 87
transportation, 84
tuberculosis, 41, 47, 48, 72

veterans, 4, 36
voter registration, 85-86

About the Contributors

Louisette A. Boucher has been a registered nurse for 25 years. She has a degree in Health Care Management from Eckerd College, St. Petersburg, Florida and a Master's degree in gerontology from the University of South Florida with a concentration in mental health counseling for older adults. During her nursing career, she organized the opening of a geriatric unit emphasizing independent care and return to prehospitalization level of functioning. She has also participated in setting up older adult community teaching programs.

Larry C. Mullins is Professor and Head, Department of Sociology, Auburn University at Montgomery. He was formerly Chair of the Department of Gerontology at the University of South Florida. While at USF, he was Program Coordinator and Acting Director of the International Exchange Center on Gerontology. He has been a visiting professor at Stockholm University in Sweden and at Free University in Amsterdam and was selected as a Gerontological Master in the Netherlands. He is an active member of the Gerontological Society of America and the Southern Gerontological Society, of which he is a past president. His research interests include health and long-term care policy and issues related to personal relations and emotional conditions of older persons.

Diane Wiatt Rich is Assistant Chair and Director of Education and Training in the Department of Aging and Mental Health at the Florida Mental Health Institute of the University of South Florida. She has Master's degrees in gerontology and German and has taught graduate and undergraduate courses in gerontology, including a course on Homelessness and Older Adults. She has experience in education and training for professionals working with older adults. She also served as Chair of the Long Range Planning Committee of the Hillsborough County Coalition for the Homeless.

Thomas A. Rich is a professor of Gerontology and Sociology at West Georgia College and was formerly Professor and Chair of Gerontology at the University of South Florida. While at USF, he also served as Dean of the College of Social and Behavioral Sciences and Director of the Center for Applied Gerontology. His research and teaching interests include gerontology, community mental health, cross-cultural studies, and the development of gerontology as a new discipline. Current interests include intervention with homeless older adults, inter-generational counseling, social policy, and mental health.

James R. Roorda has a Master's degree in gerontology from the University of South Florida. He is retired from the San Jose Police Department of San Jose, California, where he was a Field Training Officer--Psychological Services and Candidate Selection Instructor for the California State Teaching Certificate. He is currently a doctoral student in social psychology at the University of Nevada in Reno.

Judith Sullivan-Mintz is a graduate of the Department of Gerontology and has a Master's degree in counselor education from the University of South Florida. She has volunteer experience with the homeless chronically mentally ill through James A. Haley Veterans Administration Hospital and has worked as an outreach counselor with Metropolitan Ministries, Inc. of Tampa, Florida. She currently works as a drug addictions counselor.

Irena M. Zuk has a Master's degree in gerontology from the University of South Florida, with a degree concentration in mental health counseling with older adults, and a Master's degree in German from Temple University in Philadelphia, Pennsylvania. She has experience in the areas of congressional legislation, international consulting, business administration, events coordination, documentation, and teaching, and is currently working as a mental health counselor with older adults.

ISBN 0-86569-246-7
90000>
EAN
9 780865 692466
HARDCOVER BAR CODE